TEXT-CRITICAL METHODOLOGY
AND THE
PRE-CAESAREAN TEXT

STUDIES AND DOCUMENTS

Founded by Kirsopp and Silva Lake

VOLUME 43

EDITED BY

IRVING ALAN SPARKS

in Collaboration With

J. NEVILLE BIRDSALL   ELDON J. EPP
SEBASTIAN P. BROCK   GORDON D. FEE
†ERNEST CADMAN COLWELL

12.00

TEXT-CRITICAL METHODOLOGY
AND THE
PRE-CAESAREAN TEXT

Codex W in the
Gospel of Mark

BY

LARRY W. HURTADO

University of Manitoba

GRAND RAPIDS, MICHIGAN

WM. B. EERDMANS

1981

To Tiffany

Library of Congress Cataloging in Publication Data

Hurtado, Larry W   1943–
  Text-critical methodology and the pre-Caesarean
text.

  (Studies and documents; v. 43)
  A revision of the author's thesis, Case Western
Reserve University, 1973.
  Bibliography: p. 95.
  1. Bible. N.T. Mark—Criticism, Textual.
2. Bible. Manuscripts, Greek. N.T. Gospels.
Washington ms. I. Title. II. Series.
BS2585.2.H87 1981   226'.3048   80-28904
ISBN 0-8028-1872-2

PREFACE

New Testament text-critical studies are not now in vogue, and one encounters many NT scholars today for whom textual criticism is an almost totally unknown field. This is most unfortunate, for there is much to be done before we shall have a fully accurate knowledge of the history of the NT text. It is, therefore, with some concern for this much neglected line of study that I offer the research embodied here.

This book is a revised and augmented version of my Ph.D. thesis (Case Western Reserve University, 1973), and I wish to record my enormous gratitude to my supervisor, Professor Eldon Jay Epp. He gave careful attention to my work, loaned books and articles for the study from his collection, and was so helpful that his example serves as a model for my own supervision of students.

The notes in this study will reflect my indebtedness to many scholars who gave themselves energetically to research on the text of the NT. I should like to acknowledge especially the late Ernest Cadman Colwell, whose work I found particularly stimulating in my own research. The initial idea of doing this research occurred after studying the analysis of work on the Caesarean text by Bruce M. Metzger ("The Caesarean Text of the Gospels," in *Chapters in the History of New Testament Textual Criticism* [Grand Rapids: Eerdmans, 1963] 42-72). Gordon D. Fee gave helpful advice and encouragement during both the writing of the thesis and the production of the present form of the study.

I am grateful to Dr. Irving Alan Sparks and to the other members of the editorial board of Studies and Documents for accepting this work for publication, and to Dr. Edgar Smith and his colleagues at Eerdmans Publishing Company for their willingness to bring this work to press. I wish to thank Linda Block for her excellent and prompt work in typing the final manuscript, and Ted Schulz, my teaching assistant, for help in proofing. A grant from the University of Manitoba and Social Sciences and Humanities Research Council Fund Committee covered costs of preparation of the final typescript.

My wife, Shannon, helped in the revision of this work for publication, checking some of the collation work and catching several awkward turns of phrase. Her encouragement and support have been invaluable.

This book is inscribed to my daughter, Tiffany, who is still too young to understand what the work is about, but who has patiently borne with the demands on my time with her during its preparation.

Winnipeg, Manitoba   LARRY W. HURTADO
June, 1979

CONTENTS

LIST OF ABBREVIATIONS

I. TEXTUAL WITNESSES

Greek Codices

Papyrus		Century or Date
P[45]	Chester Beatty	(III)

Uncials		Century or Date
ℵ	Sinaiticus	(IV)
A	Alexandrinus	(V)
B	Vaticanus	(IV)
D	Bezae	(V/VI)
F	Boreeli	(IX)
G	Wolfii A	(IX/X)
K	Cyprius	(IX)
L	Regius	(VIII)
N	Purpureus Petropolitanus	(VI)
U	Nanianus	(IX/X)
W	Washingtonianus	(V)
X	Monacensis	(IX)
Y	Macedonianus	(IX)
Δ	Sangalliensis	(IX/X)
Θ	Koridethi	(VII-IX))
Π	Petropolitanus II	(IX)
Σ	Rossanensis	(V)
Φ	Beratinus	(VI)
Ψ	Athos, Lavra	(VIII/IX)

Minuscules (only those cited frequently)

Fam 1 Composed of MSS 1, 118, 131, and 209, all of which date from the twelfth to the fourteenth centuries.

Fam 13 Composed of MSS 13, 69, 124, 230, 346, 543, 788, 826, 828, 983, 1689, and 1709, dating from between the eleventh and fifteenth centuries.

565 Ninth or tenth century, housed in Leningrad.

700 Eleventh or twelfth century, housed at the British Museum.

1071 Twelfth century, now in the Lavra on Mount Athos.

Old Latin Witnesses

a	Vercellensis	ff	Corbeiensis
b	Veronensis	g²	Sangermanensis II
c	Colbertinus	i	Vindobonensis
d	Bezae	k	Bobbiensis
e	Palatinus	l	Rehdigeranus
f	Brixianus	n	Fragmenta Sangallensia

q	Monacensis	r²	Usserianus II
r¹	Usserianus I	aur	Codex Aureus

II. MISCELLANEOUS

Arm	Armenian Version	OL	Old Latin Version
Boh	Bohairic Coptic Version	Sah	Sahidic Coptic Version
Geo	Georgian Version	Syr	Old Syriac Versions
Goth	Gothic Version	TR	Textus Receptus
LXX	Septuagint	Vg	Vulgate
MS(S)	Manuscript(s)		

III. JOURNALS AND SCHOLARLY WORKS

AJT	*American Journal of Theology*
ATR	*Anglican Theological Review*
BBC	*Bulletin of the Bezan Club*
BDF	F. Blass, A. Debrunner, and R. W. Funk, *A Greek Grammar of the NT*
BGD	W. Bauer, F. W. Gingrich, and F. W. Danker, *A Greek-English Lexicon of the New Testament* (rev. ed. 1979)
Bib	*Biblica*
CQR	*Church Quarterly Review*
CTM	*Concordia Theological Monthly*
Est Bib	*Estudios Biblicos*
EvQ	*Evangelical Quarterly*
Exp Tim	*Expository Times*
HTR	*Harvard Theological Review*
JBL	*Journal of Biblical Literature*
JTS	*Journal of Theological Studies*
NovT	*Novum Testamentum*
NovTSup	Novum Testamentum, Supplements
NTS	*New Testament Studies*
NTTS	New Testament Tools and Studies
RB	*Revue Biblique*
RSV	*Revised Standard Version*
SD	Studies and Documents
SNTSMS	Society for New Testament Studies Monograph Series
TDNT	G. Kittel and G. Friedrich (eds.), *Theological Dictionary of the New Testament*
TextS	Texts and Studies
THKNT	Theologischer Handkommentar zum Neuen Testament
TLZ	*Theologische Literaturzeitung*

CHAPTER I
INTRODUCTION

In 1967 E. C. Colwell wrote, "The major task for the next generation of textual critics is the reassessment of the external evidence."[1] It must be agreed that this task has not been taken up on any major scale;[2] however, the present study addresses the task spoken of by Colwell and reflects the convictions that external evidence is important data for textual criticism and that a reassessment of at least some of the data is necessary.

The object of this study is a reassessment of Codex Washingtonianus in the Gospel of Mark to determine whether the standard description of the MS as the major witness of the pre-Caesarean text is correct. An important feature of this reassessment is that it employs and refines recent methodological suggestions for determining the textual relationships of MSS. Before turning to the actual data of this study, it will be helpful to discuss first the reasons for choosing to reassess Codex W, and then the reasons for and nature of the methodological advances employed here.

CODEX W AND THE CAESAREAN TEXT

The reasons for making Codex W the focus of this study have to do with its importance in connection with the Caesarean text of Mark. We do not need to review the entire history of research on the Caesarean text, as this has been done already, but it may be helpful to be reminded of the scholarly discussion that led to the now standard opinion of Codex W as a Caesarean witness.[3]

Streeter

B. H. Streeter was the first to argue that Codex W should be linked with Θ, 565, 700, and other witnesses in a group earlier identified by K. Lake and R. P. Blake.[4] Streeter also gave the name "Caesarean text" to this group, and he saw Codex W

---

[1] "External Evidence and New Testament Textual Criticism," in *Studies in the History and Text of the New Testament in Honor of Kenneth Willis Clark* (ed. B. L. Daniels and M. J. Suggs; SD 29; Salt Lake City: University of Utah, 1967) 1.

[2] See E. J. Epp, "The Twentieth Century Interlude in New Testament Textual Criticism," *JBL* 93(1974) 386-414.

[3] See the history of research by B. M. Metzger, "The Caesarean Text of the Gospels," *JBL* 64(1945) 457-89 (repr. in *Chapters in the History of New Testament Textual Criticism* [Grand Rapids: Eerdmans, 1963] 42-72).

[4] B. H. Streeter, *The Four Gospels* (2nd impression; London: Macmillan, 1926) 598-600; *idem*, "The Washington MS and the Caesarean Text of the Gospels," *JTS* 27(1926) 144-47; K. Lake and R. P. Blake, "The Text of the Gospels and the Koridethi Codex," *HTR* 16 (1923) 267-86.

as a very "pure" representative of this text and as "conclusive evidence" of a "single type of early text" represented by the Caesarean group.[5] Though subsequent studies differed on the exact nature of W's relationship with the so-called Caesarean group, Streeter's basic point that W was to be linked with Θ, 565, and the others of this group became widely accepted, as did his name for the group.[6]

Of course, the main reason that it was important whether Codex W was a Caesarean representative was that it was such an early witness (fourth or fifth century), far earlier than the other Caesareans. This meant that the Caesarean textual tradition was perhaps a very early one and that Codex W may have represented its formative stages better than the later witnesses.

The Appearance of P[45]

The publication in 1933 of P[45], the Chester Beatty Papyrus of the Gospels, served to underscore further the importance of Codex W. Kenyon's description of P[45] as Caesarean, a description that quickly came to be widely accepted, meant that the Caesarean text now had a witness even earlier (third century) than Codex W.[7] But, as Lagrange quickly showed, the agreement of P[45] with the Caesarean text was principally the agreement of P[45] with Codex W.[8] This meant that the identification of Codex W as Caesarean was the crucial matter. Further, the fragmentary condition of P[45] in Mark meant that Codex W, which showed such close agreement with P[45], was probably the most complete representative of the kind of text represented by P[45].

In the years following, the question of whether in fact Codex W and P[45] should be included in the Caesarean group received attention several times. In 1934 P. L. Hedley published a study showing that, though P[45] and Codex W seemed to exhibit a close textual relationship with each other, neither of these witnesses had many agreements with the Caesarean "archetype" of selected chapters of Mark proposed earlier by Lake, Blake, and New.[9] Hedley argued that this showed that the Caesarean witnesses did not form a unity close enough to be regarded as a distinct text-type, and he saw all the Caesareans as simply "non-neutral, Eastern" witnesses. In the same year, Lagrange published a study of P[45] noting that in Mark this MS agreed closely with Codex W, but not so well with the other Caesareans. He suggested that P[45] and W were early representatives of the textual tradition that led to the later Caesarean witnesses (such as Θ and 565), but he argued that P[45] and W formed a somewhat distinctive group of their own and could not be called Caesareans in the same sense of the word as these later witnesses.[10]

---

[5]Streeter, "The Washington MS of the Gospels," 168-69. Cf. *The Four Gospels* 599: "In Mk. 5:31–16:8, then, W is far the oldest, and much the purest, authority for this ancient and interesting type of Eastern text. . . ."

[6]E.g., K. Lake, R. P. Blake, and S. New ("The Caesarean Text of the Gospel of Mark," *HTR* 21[1928] 212 [hereafter cited as "The Caesarean Text of Mark"]) describe W as "clearly Caesarean, though not one of the best witnesses."

[7]F. G. Kenyon, *The Chester Beatty Biblical Papyri* (London: Emery Walker, 1933) I, 16.

[8]M. J. Lagrange, "Le papyrus Chester Beatty pour les Évangiles," *RB* 44(1934) 10, 17.

[9]P. L. Hedley, "The Egyptian Texts of the Gospels and Acts," *CQR* 118(1934) 23-39, 188-230, esp. 32-35. The proposed "archetype" appeared in Lake, Blake, and New, "The Caesarean Text of Mark."

[10]M. J. Lagrange, "Le papyrus Chester Beatty pour les Évangiles," 40-41.

Ayuso and the Pre-Caesarean Text

Shortly after these studies appeared, the Spanish scholar Teofilio Ayuso published an extensive article defending the "reality" and "importance" of the Caesarean text and giving special importance to P[45] and Codex W.[11] Ayuso argued that within the Caesarean group were two subgroups: one, composed of P[45], W, and weaker members including Fam 13, Fam 1, and Codex 28; and another subgroup represented mainly by Θ, 565, and 700. The former subgroup (especially P[45] and W) he saw as representing the early stage of the Caesarean text.[12] Although Lagrange had described the Caesarean MSS as exhibiting a recensional and therefore inferior text of Mark,[13] Ayuso argued that the recensional quality was restricted to the later subgroup and that the Markan text represented by P[45] and W (which he called the pre-Caesarean text) was a primitive text possessing good claims as a bearer of original Markan readings.[14] Thus, although Ayuso recognized some diversity in the Caesarean group, he defended the overall unity of the group and, by his emphasis on the value of the text of P[45] and W, made the question of their relationship to the other Caesareans all the more important.[15]

Although it is not clear to what degree Ayuso's work was known, subsequent publications began to reflect his view that the Caesarean group was made up of two subgroups. In their 1939 tribute to Lagrange, the Lakes mentioned two subgroups of Caesarean witnesses, noting that Θ, 565, and 700 agreed most often with the quotations of Mark in Origen and Eusebius and are thus the best representatives of the Caesarean text, and describing P[45] and W as the two "poorest" representatives reflecting not the Caesarean text but the text from which the Caesarean text derived.[16] In their important study on Fam 13 the Lakes again noted the two subgroups of Caesarean representatives, but instead of calling P[45] and W "poor" Caesareans, they preferred to regard these two MSS as simply "early" Caesareans representative of "a pre-Origenian" text which was "revised into the true 'Caesarean.' "[17]

Subsequent Discussion

Following the above-mentioned publications by the Lakes, most textual critics accepted the conclusion that the Caesarean group includes Codex W and P[45] as members of an early subgroup, the "pre-Caesarean" text, but the discussion did not

---

[11] "¿Texto cesariense o precesariense? su realidad y su trascendencia en la critica textual del Nuevo Testamento," *Bib* 16(1935) 369-415.

[12]Ibid., 377-78.

[13] "Le papyrus Chester Beatty pour les Évangiles."

[14] "¿Texto cesariense o precesariense?" 379-80, 384. In a later article Ayuso argued that the only two "pre-recensional" texts were the "Western" and the "pre-Caesarean" (P[45], W) and were thus the two most important bodies of witnesses for reconstructing the original NT readings. See "¿Texto arrecensional, recensional o prerecensional?" *Est Bib* segundo época 6(1947) 35-90, esp. 79-89.

[15]Later in this chapter we will return to a critique of the method Ayuso employed in his study of the agreements of the Caesarean witnesses.

[16]K. and S. Lake, "De Westcott et Hort au Pére Lagrange et au-dela," *RB* 68(1939) 503.

[17]K. and S. Lake, *Family 13 (the Ferrar Group): The Text According to Mark* (SD 11; London: Christophers, 1941) 7-8 (hereafter cited as *Family 13*). See also S. Lake, *Family Pi and the Codex Alexandrinus* (SD 5; London: Christophers, 1937) 4, 62-64.

end. E. F. Hills, in his 1946 dissertation on the Caesarean group, argued for a threefold grouping of the witnesses; he placed Θ, 565, and 700 in one subgroup, Fam 1, Fam 13, and Codex 28 in another subgroup, and Codex W "in a class by itself . . . a third group."[18] Several years later, Hollis Huston published a study arguing that, though P[45] and W showed many agreements with each other, neither supported the other Caesarean witnesses enough to be classified as Caesarean. He also rejected the description of P[45] and W as "pre-Caesarean" because the term implies that "this earlier form of the text has a unique relationship with the Caesarean text . . . while the evidence cited above does not bear out this relationship."[19]

There is also evidence that the Lakes themselves may have begun to question their earlier views about the unity of the Caesarean group. Their 1928 article, which gave a "reconstructed" Caesarean text of Mark 1, 6, and 11, was intended originally as only a preliminary publication, and a proposed reconstruction of the whole of the supposed archetype of the Caesarean group was to follow.[20] As late as 1941 the Lakes still wrote of the future publication of this work, but they also mentioned the need for a "complete rewriting" of nearly finished work in view of newer data.[21] The publication never appeared, and no clear reason was given; but, in a 1946 letter to H. J. Cadbury, S. Lake wrote that by then she had come to regard the two "sub-groups" of Caesarean witnesses as "so distinct that they represent two distinct textual types."[22]

The present situation is therefore somewhat confusing. On the one hand, since 1939 scholars have been writing about the disintegration of the Caesarean group.[23] On the other hand, scholars continue to treat the Caesarean text as an established and important grouping of witnesses.[24] In particular, the view that Codex W and P[45] are Markan representatives of the Caesarean text is nearly standard opinion.[25] The above discussion shows, however, that it would be helpful to look again at the textual relationships of these MSS to see whether they are legitimately to be regarded as related to Caesarean witnesses such as Θ and 565. Because P[45]

[18]"The Caesarean Family of New Testament Manuscripts" (Th.D. dissertation, Harvard Divinity School, 1946) 25-26, 30-31, 80. See also Hills, "The Inter-Relationship of the Caesarean Manuscripts," *JBL* 68(1949) 141-59. He made no mention of the place of P[45] in these groups.

[19]H. W. Huston, "Mark 6 and 11 in P[45] and in the Caesarean Text," *JBL* 74(1955) 270.

[20]S. Lake wrote (*Family Pi and the Codex Alexandrinus*, 60 n. 12), "Such a reconstruction has, however, been prepared by K. and S. Lake and will *hoffentlich* be published in 1937."

[21]K. and S. Lake, *Family 13* 8.

[22]The letter, dated Oct. 18, 1946, is referred to by J. H. Greenlee, *The Gospel Text of Cyril of Jerusalem* (SD 17; Copenhagen: Munksgaard, 1955) 13. Note the reference to delay of the reconstructed text of Mark in A. H. White, "The Problem of the Caesarean Text," *Journal of the Manchester University Egypt and Oriental Society* 24(1942-45; published in 1947) 41.

[23]C. C. Tarelli, "The Chester Beatty Papyrus and the Caesarean Text," *JTS* 40(1939) 49; also A. H. White, "The Problem of the Caesarean Text," 51-55; Metzger, "The Caesarean Text of the Gospels," 67.

[24]See, e.g., B. M. Metzger, *The Text of the New Testament* (2nd ed.; New York/London: Oxford University, 1968) 214-15. See J. H. Greenlee (*The Gospel Text of Cyril of Jerusalem* 32), who notes the division of the Caesarean group; but, when he finds Cyril closer to the "pre-Caesarean" MSS, he still calls Cyril's quotations "clearly Caesarean." See also M. M. Carder, "A Caesarean Text in the Catholic Epistles," *NTS* 16(1969-70) 252-70; K. Aland, "Bemerkungen zu den gegenwärtigen Möglichkeiten textkritischer Arbeit aus Anlass einer Untersuchung zum Cäsareatext der Katholischer Briefe," *NTS* 17(1970-71) 1-9.

[25]E.g., Metzger, *The Text of the New Testament* 37, 56-57.

is so fragmentary in Mark, we have chosen to give attention to Codex W as the more extensive representative of the so-called pre-Caesarean text.

THE METHODOLOGICAL PROBLEM

The major problem in the discussion of whether the Caesarean witnesses formed a sufficiently homogeneous group to be regarded as a text-type was that no one had formulated an adequate definition of a text-type relationship, nor had anyone determined an adequate method for discovering such a relationship between two or more witnesses.

Agreement in Non-Byzantine Readings

Initially, the method used in studying textual relationships was to count agreements of MSS in variations from the TR. Because it was believed that the "Byzantine Text" (represented by the TR) was a recension made in the fifth or sixth century that became the standard text by which non-Byzantine MSS were revised, readings not supported by the Byzantine text were regarded as remnants of earlier text-types. By tabulating agreements of MSS in these readings one could determine genealogical relationships, and many agreements between two witnesses in these readings suggested that the two belonged to the same textual group.[26]

In his work on the Caesarean MSS Streeter ignored the frequent agreements of these witnesses with the TR, insisting that these agreements showed only that these MSS and/or their "ancestors" had suffered revision under the influence of the Byzantine text in varying places in the Gospels and to varying degrees.[27] Indeed, Streeter seems to have regarded almost any amount of agreement in non-Byzantine readings as evidence of a textual relationship, and because of this he felt he was able to add numerous MSS to the Caesarean group.[28]

It may seem strange, but there was no objective criterion for *sufficient* agreement to show two witnesses to be members of the same group. Furthermore, scholars usually paid little attention to the amount of disagreement between MSS. That is, they seem not to have seen the importance of studying *agreement in relation to disagreement* of two MSS. For example, if two MSS agree fifty times in variants from the TR, but one of them has another sixty variants from the TR not shared by the other MS, how significant is the number of agreements of these two MSS?

It is clear that conclusions about textual relationships of MSS based on the counting of non-Byzantine readings as described here must be regarded as highly tenuous, and it is clear, too, that a reevaluation of MSS by use of a better method is necessary. Not only were such counts practically meaningless, but the whole procedure of considering "non-Byzantine" readings was severely shaken by the

---

[26]This method was used, e.g., by K. Lake, *Codex 1 of the Gospels and Its Allies* (TextS VII/3; Cambridge: Cambridge University, 1902) xxiii-xxiv; and by K. Lake, R. P. Blake, and S. New, "The Caesarean Text of Mark."

[27]Streeter, *The Four Gospels* 81-82.

[28]Streeter, "Origen, ‭א‬ and the Caesarean Text," *JTS* 36(1935) 178-79; *idem*, "Codices 157, 1071 and the Caesarean Text," *Quantulacumque, Studies Presented to Kirsopp Lake* (ed. R. P. Casey, S. Lake, and A. K. Lake; London: Christophers, 1937) 149-50.

study of P[45]. Though the "Byzantine" readings in MSS like Codex W had been disregarded and seen merely as evidence of early Byzantine revisions, in P[45], a papyrus too early (third century) to have been revised by a Byzantine standard text, scholars found numerous readings previously regarded as Byzantine readings. Streeter and the Lakes had argued that, when Caesarean witnesses disagreed, some supporting a reading found in the TR and others supporting one or more other readings, one of the non-Byzantine readings was the original "Caesarean text-type" reading and the agreements with the TR showed where Caesarean MSS had suffered Byzantine revisions that disturbed an earlier unity of readings. P[45] showed, however, many "Byzantine" readings that could not have been "revised" into the text of P[45] from a Byzantine MS. Thus, major reasons for doubt arose about the unity of the Caesarean group. As Hedley stated, "P[45] makes it clear that the plan of editing 'the Caesarean text' by amalgamating the variants of Θ and its friends from TR may produce something useful, but will create something that never existed."[29]

Methods Used in Other Studies

Both critics and supporters of the Caesarean text-type realized the fallacies in the earlier work. Ayuso, a supporter, knew that the Lakes' procedure for reconstructing the Caesarean archetype was a failure and did not himself try to reconstruct an archetype. His only concern was to prove that such an archetypal text lay behind the Caesarean witnesses by trying to show that these witnesses were, in fact, a somewhat homogeneous group.[30] For this task Ayuso offered a method for isolating readings that he termed *propias* and *exclusivas*. By the former term he meant readings that were not sufficiently supported by important witnesses of any other text-type to label the readings as belonging to some non-Caesarean text-type. By *exclusivas* he meant readings that were supported *only* by witnesses generally regarded as members of the Caesarean group. By drawing up lists of such readings in both categories, Ayuso tried to demonstrate the textual relationships of the Caesarean group.

We have already noted that Ayuso proposed a bifurcation of the Caesarean group into an early subgroup (Codex W, P[45], Fam 13 as primary members) and a later subgroup (Θ, 565, 700 as primary members), and his work deserves some further discussion because, though it has been cited as important, few scholars seem to have analyzed his study closely.[31] Close analysis of his work shows some important methodological weaknesses.

First, in drawing up the list of readings which he offered as Caesarean, Ayuso seems to have taken too lightly the support which many of these readings receive from OL MSS or other witnesses. His concern was whether readings were

---

[29]P. L. Hedley, "The Egyptian Texts of the Gospels and Acts," 33-34, also 35, 222. See also Lagrange, "Le papyrus Chester Beatty pour les Évangiles," 21; *idem*, "Le group dit césaréen des manuscrits des Évangiles," *RB* 38(1929) 511; Tarelli, "The Chester Beatty Papyrus and the Caesarean Text," 51-52.

[30]Ayuso, "¿Texto cesariense o precesariense?" 386-87.

[31]See Metzger, "The Caesarean Text of the Gospels," 67; *idem*, "Recent Spanish Contributions to the Textual Criticism of the New Testament," *Chapters in the History of New Testament Textual Criticism* 121, 124-25. The major reason may be that Ayuso published his work in Spanish.

supported by "major" witnesses such as א, B, or D. Although these are the leading Greek representatives of the Neutral and Western textual groups, the lack of their support is not a fully trustworthy indication that a reading does not belong to one or the other of the textual traditions they represent.[32] For example, in view of the lack of homogeneity in the Western text, it is not proper to think that D is always a fully representative witness of Western readings, nor is it correct to think that at a given place in Mark only one reading can be called *the* Western reading. This means that many of Ayuso's *propias* readings that are supported by a few OL MSS or by other witnesses may be "Western" readings and not really distinctive Caesarean readings at all.

Second, Ayuso gave no indication of how his list of Caesarean readings compares in number with comparable lists of distinctively Neutral, Byzantine, or Western readings. It is not agreement of any kind that displays textual relationship, but agreements that can be shown to be numerous by some legitimate standard of comparison.

Third, Ayuso did not analyze the *kind* of variants that he listed as proof of Caesarean relationship. He did not consider the chance of agreements due to such obvious and common causes as coincidental harmonizations of Mark with the other Gospels, and coincidental stylistic changes in Mark.[33] These methodological flaws in Ayuso's work are sufficient reason to call into question his conclusions.

In the same period as Ayuso, J. Baikie employed another approach to studying the textual relationships of the Caesarean witnesses, but his method too must be judged inadequate.[34] Baikie selected Matthew 3, Mark 12, and Luke 12 as sample chapters, studying the agreements of the Caesarean MSS under a wide variety of categories of readings. After looking at the agreements of the Caesarean witnesses with one another and their agreements with non-Caesarean witnesses, Baikie found some "unswerving associations" in certain categories of readings, such as the associations of 565 with Θ, and, at times, W with Fam 1 and 28. His overall conclusion, however, was that, while there is evidence of common textual *influences* upon the Caesarean MSS in diverse ways, he was unconvinced that there was a unity of origin or that the Caesarean MSS showed a close relationship.[35]

Baikie's study did mark an advance upon earlier work in that he attempted both to analyze the *kind* of variants supported by the Caesareans and to indicate the amount of agreement of the Caesarean MSS with one another in comparison with their agreement with non-Caesarean witnesses. But his selection of such a small amount of text to be studied (only three chapters from the Synoptic Gospels!) makes his conclusions somewhat less than convincing.

E. F. Hills, in the study mentioned above and in his published articles, employed a method of "random sampling," which consisted of determining the percentage of agreement of two MSS at points in the text of Mark where both MSS

---

[32]Cf. Ayuso, "¿Texto cesariense o precesariense?" 387, 402, 409.

[33]The only discrimination used by Ayuso was the elimination of itacisms; see ibid., 387.

[34]James E. McA. Baikie, "The Caesarean Text *Inter Pares*" (M. Litt. dissertation, Cambridge University, 1936). The work was done under F. C. Burkitt. A summary is given by Metzger, "The Caesarean Text of the Gospels," 59. I used a microfilm copy of Baikie's manuscript.

[35]Baikie, "The Caesarean Text *Inter Pares*," 214, 233, 240, 251-54. One is reminded of Hedley's words about the relationship of the Caesareans to one another: "I admit affinity, but deny consanguinity" ("The Egyptian Texts of the Gospels and Acts," 225).

vary from the TR reading. This procedure gives some idea of the amount of agreement in comparison to disagreement, but the exclusion of "Byzantine" readings gives a distorted picture of the textual complexion of a MS.[36]

The clear conclusion that arises from this brief examination of previous methods used in the study of the relationships of the Caesarean witnesses is that none of the previous studies has employed a method that would yield objective and firm answers. For this reason, the present study will reexamine the relationship of Codex W to the other Caesareans (a matter whose importance has been described above) by means of a methodological advance upon previous studies.

THE NATURE OF THE PRESENT STUDY

At this point it will be proper to describe the nature of the present study in some detail. Before we examine the approach here followed, however, let us summarize the results of the preceding discussion in order that the description of this study may be seen in the clearest light.

The Choice of Codex W

We have seen above that a persistent question in the debate on the Caesarean text was whether Codex W was to be included as a member of this group. Though everyone seems to have agreed that Codex W and P[45] show close agreement with each other, and though the view became dominant that these two MSS are chief witnesses of a text form that is an early stage of the Caesarean text (represented by Θ, 565, and 700), there were objections.

The significance of this debate is considerable for NT textual criticism. If Codex W and P[45] are early Caesareans in Mark, then the Caesarean text is a very primitive and important text-type. If they are not Caesareans, then the Caesarean text may be only a later development in Markan textual tradition. If these witnesses are not Caesarean, then to what textual group do they belong? Might not the textual history of Mark need to be rewritten if these witnesses have been incorrectly identified?

We have chosen to focus on Codex W because it is the more extensive of the two major "pre-Caesareans." If the standard view is correct that W and P[45] represent basically the same text (although we shall test this), then conclusions about the textual relationships of Codex W will legitimately apply to the two of them and to the so-called pre-Caesarean text as a whole.

The Emphasis on a New Method

This study is as much an argument for proper method in determining textual relationships as it is an examination of Codex W, for we have seen above that previous

---

[36]Cf. Hills, "The Caesarean Family of New Testament Manuscripts," 1-22; *idem*, "The Inter-Relationships of the Caesarean Manuscripts," 151-52. These two works also treat the history of methods used in grouping MSS up to Hills's time.

work had such serious methodological shortcomings that some advance in method is necessary. Let us briefly summarize these shortcomings.

First, it is obvious that the counting of "non-Byzantine" readings is an insufficient basis for deciding textual relationships, and for some time scholars have been calling for a better method.[37] It is clearly better to study MSS as they are, without "scraping off" theoretical Byzantine revisions.

Second, it is meaningless to give counts of agreements between MSS without some means of showing objectively how much agreement is indicative of a close textual relationship. In research on the Caesarean text, sometimes questionably small amounts of agreement were used as evidence of a group relationship.[38] In other words, earlier studies had no criterion of quantitative agreement.

Third, insufficient attention was given to the *kind* of agreements of MSS. In particular, scholars often failed to ask whether agreements might be merely coincidental and of little significance for showing textual relationships.[39] That is, in the same way that a textual relationship is not indicated unless there is a significant *amount* of agreement, so there must be significant *kinds* of agreements to demonstrate a textual relationship.

Fourth, inadequate attention given to the kinds of readings shared by the Caesareans made it difficult to gain consent as to the kind or quality of text attested by these witnesses. Some characterized the Caesarean MSS as exhibiting a text of inferior quality, with many harmonizations of Mark with the other Gospels.[40] Ayuso argued vigorously that the "pre-Caesarean" text (W, P[45]) was free of these characteristics, but gave no thorough analysis of readings to support his argument.[41] Colwell has urged a clearer definition of what kind of text the Caesareans represent, and has characterized Streeter's vague description—a text "equidistant from both the Alexandrian and Western texts"[42]—as so many "weasel words."[43] Klijn, too, refers to the lack of study on the quality of the Caesarean text, noting "and here we hit on the real difficulty of this text: nobody can describe what kind of text the Caesarean really represents."[44]

Finally, much previous work must be considered inconclusive on account of the procedure of studying "samples" of a MS. In some cases scholars attempted to make the samples as representative as they could;[45] but it is now clear that

[37]See, e.g., Metzger, "The Caesarean Text of the Gospels," 70; H. R. Murphy, "Eusebius' New Testament Text in *Demonstratio Evangelica*," *JBL* 73(1954) 167-68.

[38]In criticizing the use of such counts of non-Byzantine agreements, E. C. Colwell wrote, "Nowhere was this method followed more disastrously than in Streeter's elaboration of Lake's work on the Caesarean text" (*Studies in Methodology in Textual Criticism of the New Testament* [Grand Rapids: Eerdmans, 1969] 4).

[39]Note similar comments in Metzger, "The Caesarean Text of the Gospels," 71-72, e.g., "But it seems to the present writer that the possibility of mere chance coincidence among manuscripts in agreeing in small variations . . . has not been sufficiently taken into account."

[40]Hedley, "The Egyptian Texts of the Gospels and Acts"; Lagrange, "Le papyrus Chester Beatty pour les Évangiles," 19; Baikie, "The Caesarean Text *Inter Pares*"; Hills, "The Caesarean Family of New Testament Manuscripts," 80; *idem*, "The Inter-Relationship of the Caesarean Manuscripts," 155-56, 158.

[41]"¿Texto cesariense o precesariense?" 379-80, 384.

[42]Streeter, *The Four Gospels* 84.

[43]Colwell, *Studies in Methodology* 36-37.

[44]A. F. J. Klijn, *A Survey of the Researches into the Western Text of the Gospels and Acts: Part Two 1949-1969* (NovTSup 21; Leiden: E. J. Brill, 1969) 34-35.

[45]E.g., Lake, Blake, New ("The Caesarean Text of Mark"), who selected Mark 1, 6, 11.

important MSS should be studied over the entire text of a biblical book, and that agreements should be tabulated not only for the entire portion of the text but also chapter by chapter, for some MSS show differing textual affiliations in different portions of the same biblical book.[46] In studying the Caesarean witnesses, one obviously ought to study agreements chapter by chapter over the entirety of the Gospel of Mark.

With these criticisms of previous studies in mind let us now examine the method employed in the present study.

The Method Used

Our purpose in this study is to examine the textual relationships and complexion of Codex W in Mark in order to ascertain whether W agrees closely enough with the major Caesarean witnesses, Θ and 565, to be considered a representative of an early stage of the Caesarean text. A second but important question to be dealt with is the *kind* of Markan text W exhibits. Colwell described the "scribal habits" of P[45] as attempts at concise expression, clarity, and good Koine style.[47] We shall attempt to characterize the distinctive readings of W to see if it too exhibits an "edited" text of Mark.

The approach taken here for determining textual relationships involves a quantitative description of textual relationships and an examination of the kind of readings shared by two witnesses. The method for determining quantitative relationships of MSS first developed by Colwell and Tune is used here with certain refinements.[48]

(a) Essential to the method is the selection of representative witnesses from each major textual grouping; these witnesses are collated, together with the MS one seeks to study, over a large amount of biblical text, and all variations among them are noted, not just variations from an external textual standard such as the TR.[49] The relationship of the MS being studied to the representatives of each major group indicates whether the MS is to be placed in one of the groups.

(b) The points in the text where variant readings occur are called "variation-units," and the quantitative relationship of any two MSS can be expressed as the percentage of the total number of variation-units at which the two MSS have the same reading or "variant."[50]

(c) A large body of text must be studied, preferably a whole book of the NT. Further, the counting of agreements should be done chapter by chapter in order

[46]See, e.g., G. D. Fee, "Codex Sinaiticus in the Gospel of John: A Contribution to Methodology in Establishing Textual Relationships," *NTS* 15(1968-69) 23-44.

[47]E. C. Colwell, *Studies in Methodology* 106-24.

[48]E. C. Colwell, *Studies in Methodology* 56-62. See also G. D. Fee, "Codex Sinaiticus in the Gospel of John," 23-44, who employed the same method with "refinements" similar to those used in the present work. See a brief description of the basic method and its antecedents in E. J. Epp, "The Twentieth Century Interlude in New Testament Textual Criticism," *JBL* 93(1974) 408-9.

[49]Though it would be ideal to collate a MS against all other textual witnesses, this is of course impossible.

[50]E. J. Epp ("Toward a Clarification of the Term 'Textual Variant,' " *Studies in New Testament Language and Text: Essays in Honour of George D. Kilpatrick on the Occasion of his Sixty-fifth Birthday* [ed. J. K. Elliott; Leiden: E. J. Brill, 1976] 153-73) has made a helpful attempt to clarify the language of textual criticism, and it is to be hoped that his suggestions will receive acceptance.

to detect any shift in the textual relationship of witnesses from one part of a book to another. This study covers the agreements of the witnesses chosen throughout the whole of the Gospel of Mark and shows the agreements of witnesses chapter by chapter.

(d) All variation-units in which the only variant reading is supported by only one of the MSS are not included in the tabulation because the object of the study is to measure the comparative *agreement* of each MS with each of the others. The variation-units where only one MS has a singular reading show only that at those points the MS does not agree with the other witnesses. Also variation-units do not show group relationships when, among witnesses from the major text groups, all but one have the same reading.

(e) The agreements of each possible pairing of MSS are counted, and these counts are converted into percentages of the total number of variation-units accepted for study. Thus one can compare the quantitative agreement (expressed in percentage of variation-units) of any pair of MSS with the agreement of all other pairs, and this in turn allows one to interpret the percentage of agreement of MSS as either comparatively significant or insignificant. For example, in the present study the two witnesses of the Neutral text, ℵ and B, never show a chapter by chapter agreement of less than 71 percent, and their agreement is always at least 12 percentage points greater than the agreement of either with any of the other witnesses studied. The agreement of the two Byzantine witnesses, A and TR, is never less than 72.6 percent, and their agreement is always at least 19 percentage points higher than the agreement of either with any other witness. Therefore, if the quantitative relationship of ℵ to B or A to TR is indicative of a text-type relationship, we can say that two witnesses which do not show a similar "pattern" of quantitative agreement do not appear to be members of the same text-type. That is, the quantitative definition of a text-type relationship would appear to be an agreement that is about 70 percent or more and is at the same time about 10 percentage points or more greater than the quantitative relationship of either with witnesses outside the text-type.[51]

(f) Colwell and Tune suggested the "weighing" of variants according to their significance before counting them, and advocated the ignoring of agreements that were not "significant." In this study we shall defer the valuing of variants until after the counting of agreements in order to avoid as much as possible any subjectivity in determining the quantitative relationship of MSS. We shall examine and "weigh" the significance of particular agreements in an effort to clarify the textual relationship of two witnesses *after their quantitative relationship has been determined*.[52] Since the object of this study is to determine whether Codex W is related to the Caesarean text, we will examine the individual agreements of W with Codex Θ and 565, and with other possible allies (D, Fam 13, P[45]), in an attempt to determine whether these agreements are significant for demonstrating a textual relationship.

[51]In their article proposing the basic method followed here, Colwell and Tune propose basically the same quantitative definition of a text-type relationship (Colwell, *Studies in Methodology* 59). Thus the present study seems to corroborate their suggested definition.

[52]Cf. Colwell, *Studies in Methodology* 57. G. D. Fee (*Papyrus Bodmer II*) (P66): Its Textual *Relationships and Scribal Characteristics* [SD 34; Salt Lake City: University of Utah, 1968]; "Codex Sinaiticus in the Gospel of John") used the same method employed in the present study and also departs from Colwell in this procedure.

The above procedure, then, involves both a comparative quantitative description of the textual relationships of a witness and a description of the kinds of agreements of a witness with other witnesses. Having described the method used in this study, we will now set forth the advantages of the method over previous approaches.

(a) This method involves the counting of agreements of two witnesses at all points where the witnesses used in the study show groupings around variants, not just where the witnesses vary from the TR. One thereby is able to study the relationship of one witness with another over their entire texts.

(b) The quantitative relationship of any two witnesses can be interpreted as significant or insignificant by means of one's ability to compare the quantitative relationships of all the witnesses used in the study. Subjectivity is thus removed from evaluation of the quantitative agreement of two witnesses.

(c) The "weighing" of agreements after determining quantitative relationships allows one to say something about the kind of agreements two witnesses share: e.g., whether the agreements are unique to them or supported by other witnesses, and whether the agreements can be explained as coincidences or appear to demand some kind of textual relationship.

(d) By studying the whole of a NT book, or a similarly large body of text, one avoids the danger of "sampling" the text of witnesses.

The Witnesses Used

The witnesses used in this study were selected in order to provide a convincing answer to the question of whether Codex W shows a special affinity for the Caesarean text. Codex Vaticanus (B) and Codex Sinaiticus (ℵ) were selected as chief witnesses of the Neutral text. Codex Bezae (D) is the best Greek representative of the Western text.[53] Codex Alexandrinus (A) represents an early form of the Byzantine text in Mark, and the Textus Receptus (TR) represents the late form of this text-type.[54]

To determine the relationship of W to the Caesarean text, Codex Koridethi (Θ) and 565 were selected as representatives of the theoretically later form of the text. Fam 13, the reconstructed text by K. and S. Lake, was used to see if this witness is indeed an ally of Codex W, as is widely believed. P[45] is also included in this study, but only in a limited section because the papyrus is so fragmentary in Mark. The most intact portions used here are 6:37-48; 7:4-10; 7:25-35; 8:11-23; 8:36–9:5; 9:19-29.

---

[53]For basic data on Codex Bezae, see Metzger, *The Text of the New Testament* 49-50. On the connection of Codex Bezae to the early Western text, see E. J. Epp, "The 'Ignorance Motif' in Acts and Anti-Judaic Tendencies in Codex Bezae," *HTR* 55(1962) 52 n. 12; *idem*, "Coptic Manuscript G67 and the Role of Codex Bezae as a Western Witness in Acts," *JBL* 85(1966) 197-212; *idem, The Theological Tendency of Codex Bezae Cantabrigiensis in Acts* (SNTSMS 3; Cambridge: Cambridge University, 1966) 7-27.

[54]The evolution of the Byzantine text-type is described by K. and S. Lake, "The Byzantine Text of the Gospels," *Mémorial Lagrange* (Paris, 1940) 251-58; here they describe Family Pi as a form of the text earlier than Codex A. Prof. Paul McReynolds, who has specialized in studying the Byzantine text, suggests in a letter to the present writer that Codex A may be the earlier form.

SUMMARY

Many questions are connected with the Caesarean text, but this study is specifically limited to determining whether Codex W and the text it represents in Mark are closely related to the Caesarean text as represented by Θ and 565, i.e., whether Codex W is a "pre-Caesarean" witness representing an early stage of the Caesarean text.

In the foregoing pages we have noted that because of the fragmentary condition of P[45], the question of whether the Caesarean text is an early or later text-type can be determined by examining the textual relationships of Codex W. Further, we have found good reason to make this examination because of the methodological flaws in previous studies. In the following chapters, therefore, we will look first at the relationship between W and the Western text, with which Codex W seems to have many agreements in the early chapters of Mark. Then we will examine the relationship of W with the Caesarean representatives mentioned above (Θ, 565). After looking at the relationships of W with Fam 13 and with P[45], we will finally look at the "singular" readings in W in order to define the editorial or scribal purposes that they seem to reflect.

CHAPTER II

CODEX W AND THE WESTERN TEXT

While Codex W is known primarily as an early Caesarean witness, it is also common knowledge among textual critics that W shows some alignment with the "Western text," especially in the first few chapters of Mark. This chapter will give brief attention to the extent of Western agreement in W. We shall not study individual agreements but only the quantitative relationship of W and the Western text in Mark. That W is predominantly "Western" in the early part of Mark is not contested in this study. Nor is there an attempt made here to add to knowledge of the nature of "Western readings." In this chapter we have two purposes. First, we wish to try to determine in more objective quantitative terms how much Western affiliation there is in W, and we wish to show where this Western affiliation in W is quantitatively strongest. It will be noted that the textual "break" in W, at which point Western agreements cease to be predominant, appears to be somewhat earlier in Mark than the traditionally accepted point (Mark 5:31).

Second, we wish to show that a significant percentage of Western agreement in W continues throughout the whole of Mark. We will show, in Chapter III of this study, that these Western agreements considerably help to explain the agreement of W with Θ and 565, the representatives of the Caesarean text.

Thus for this study the Western agreement in W is studied only as it throws light on the more important question of W's relationship with the Caesarean text.

PREVIOUS RESEARCH

Sanders viewed Mark 1:1–5:30 as especially allied with the Western text. He emphasized the agreement of W there with the OL MSS, and he explained how W came to show such agreement with these OL witnesses by the hypothesis that a trilingual MS lay in the ancestry of W.[1] The Greek of W, he theorized, had been influenced by a kind of reverse translation via this trilingual MS. Years ago F. C. Burkitt took Sanders to task for these views and showed fallacies in Sanders's procedures.[2]

Theories of Latin influence upon Greek texts were once more popular than today, but present-day textual critics are less inclined to see such influence because many similarities between a Greek MS and a Latin MS can be shown to have resulted from independent attempts of copyists and translators to make the text more

---

[1]Henry A. Sanders, *The New Testament Manuscripts in the Freer Collection* (New York: Macmillan, 1912, 1918) 63-74.

[2]"W and Θ: Studies in the Western Text of St. Mark," *JTS* 17(1916) 5-6.

clear and understandable. Furthermore, it is equally possible, if not more so, that Greek readings influenced the versional readings rather than vice versa. This seems all the more likely with the discovery of numerous early papyri, with many readings heretofore attested mainly in OL MSS or other versions.[3] It is doubtful that these papyri readings were influenced by any version.

The determining of agreements between a Greek MS and the OL or any version is a procedure requiring a mastery of the particular language of the version. Even then the process is to be carried out with caution. The present writer's limited familiarity with Latin disallowed precise judgments on the degree of W's affinity with this version. It is possible, however, to judge the relationship of W with D, the best Greek representative of the Western textual tradition.

Although his view on the process by which W came to have its Western readings has been rejected, Sanders's division of the Markan text of W at 5:31, with the text to this point being clearly Western and the part of Mark after this point being much less so, is widely accepted.[4] Sanders employed no really clear method in determining the extent of Western affiliation, and he gave no exact defense for his breaking of the Markan text at 5:31. Later, E. F. Hills included in his dissertation some comments on the text of W. His conclusions were (1) that W has a stronger relationship with the Western text in Mark 1–4 only, and (2) that in any case the Western agreement in W, even in these early chapters, was not enough to alter the "fundamentally Caesarean character of the text."[5]

With the use of the Colwell-Tune quantitative method it will be possible to show the strength of W's relationship with the Western text in comparison with W's other relationships. We shall thus be able to say whether W is strongly and clearly Western or "fundamentally Caesarean" in the first part of Mark.

THE DATA

Mark 1–4

We shall now discuss the data on W's relationship with the Western text in Mark, looking first at the data for Mark 1–4 where this Western relationship is strongest. Then, more briefly, we shall discuss Mark 5–16. It must be noted here that nowhere in Mark does W show an agreement of 70 percent or more with any witness from the major text-types. W cannot, therefore, easily be classified with any established text-type. We shall note, however, the witnesses with which W agrees most often.

In Mark 1 W has no very close ally. The relationship of W with D is about the same as that of W with the Byzantine MSS. Here are the quantitative relationships of W in Mark 1.[6]

---

[3]See E. C. Colwell's caution on the excessive reliance on versions for textual evidence (*Studies in Methodology* 7-8); also E. J. Epp (*Theological Tendency* 8-9), as the theory of Latinization applies to Codex D. On Latin versions see B. M. Metzger, *The Early Versions of the New Testament: Their Origin, Transmission and Limitations* (Oxford: Clarendon, 1977) 285-374.

[4]Sanders, *The New Testament Manuscripts in the Freer Collection* 73-74.

[5]"The Caesarean Family of New Testament Manuscripts," 64-65.

[6]For the full relationship of all MSS used, see the tables in Appendix I.

```
W-TR  = 48.9%
W-D   = 44.3%
W-A   = 43.2%
W-Θ   = 43.2%
W-B   = 38.6%
W-565 = 34.1%
W-13  = 33.0%
W-ℵ   = 30.7%
```

A glance at D's quantitative relationships shows that W and Θ are D's two closest allies.

```
D-Θ   = 48.7%
D-W   = 44.3%
D-B   = 42.1%
D-13  = 38.6%
D-TR  = 37.5%
D-A   = 36.4%
D-565 = 35.2%
D-ℵ   = 34.1%
```

This confirms that W has a streak of Western readings in Mark 1. It is not clear, however, that W's Western affinity is predominant here.

In Mark 2 the data yield a clearer picture.

```
W-D   = 46.8%
W-ℵ   = 34.8%
W-B   = 30.4%
W-A   = 27.5%
W-TR  = 26.1%
W-Θ   = 26.1%
W-565 = 24.6%
W-13  = 23.2%
```

Here W's relationship with D is not overwhelmingly close (46.8%), but it is clearly stronger than the relationship of W with any other control witness. Note that W's relationship with the Byzantine witnesses (A, TR) is decidedly weaker than in Mark 1. From the standpoint of D, Codex W is by far the closest ally.

```
D-W   = 46.8%
D-Θ   = 36.2%
D-565 = 36.2%
D-13  = 34.8%
D-ℵ   = 33.3%
D-A   = 31.9%
D-TR  = 30.4%
D-B   = 27.5%
```

Here in Mark 2 it is safe to say that W's Western relationship is pronounced in comparison with W's other relationships.

16

In Mark 3 W and D continue to share a quantitative relationship significantly stronger than their relationships with the other witnesses.

W-D	=	46.9%	D-W	=	46.9%
W-ℵ	=	28.1%	D-13	=	34.4%
W-Θ	=	28.1%	D-Θ	=	32.8%
W-13	=	28.1%	D-A	=	32.8%
W-B	=	28.1%	D-565	=	29.7%
W-565	=	25.0%	D-ℵ	=	29.7%
W-A	=	23.4%	D-TR	=	28.1%
W-TR	=	23.4%	D-B	=	21.9%

The gap separating the W-D relationship from W's next closest agreement is over 18 percentage points. So, while W is not easily identified as a primary Western witness here, W's relationship with the Western text is clearly stronger than its relationship with any other textual group.

In Mark 4 the strength of W's alliance with D rises to its high-water mark for the entire Gospel.

W-D	=	57.9%
W-Θ	=	42.1%
W-13	=	35.8%
W-565	=	34.7%
W-B	=	27.4%
W-A	=	26.3%
W-ℵ	=	25.3%
W-TR	=	23.2%

The next closest ally for W is Θ, but the gap between the W-D agreement and the W-Θ agreement is 15 percentage points, making the W-Θ relationship not a significant quantitative relationship.

For D the closest relationship is with W, but 565 appears here as a close second.

D-W	=	57.9%
D-565	=	53.7%
D-Θ	=	46.3%
D-13	=	30.5%
D-TR	=	27.4%
D-B	=	27.4%
D-ℵ	=	25.3%
D-A	=	23.2%

In Mark 1–4 as a block, then, and especially in Mark 2–4, W's alliance with D (the Western witness) is clearly stronger than W's agreement with any Neutral, Byzantine, or Caesarean witness. Indeed, W and Fam 13 show no conspicuous quantitative relationship at all here. W shows noticeably closer agreement with Θ or 565 only when these witnesses are in comparatively closer agreement with D. This matter is discussed at greater length in the next chapter, where W's relationship with Θ is the topic. It seems, however, that Hills was incorrect when he called Codex W "fundamentally Caesarean" in these chapters. Rather, judged by its relationship to D, W is noticeably closer to the Western text in this part of Mark.

Mark 5

Mark 5 shows a decided change in the textual relationships of W.

W-13	=	48.8%
W-A	=	47.6%
W-B	=	45.2%
W-TR	=	42.9%
W-ℵ	=	42.9%
W-565	=	36.9%
W-Θ	=	33.3%
W-D	=	27.4%

A tabulation of W's agreements with D in Mark 5:1-30, where, according to Sanders, W is still clearly Western, shows only a 34.4 percent agreement. When one compares this figure with that for the relationship of W with D in Mark 4 (57.9%), it seems that even within Mark 5:1-30 there is a change in W's textual relationships. The point at which W ceases to be heavily Western is earlier than 5:31, where most scholars, following Sanders's conclusions, place it.

We may pause to note a few specific agreements in Mark 5:1-6 at this point. In 5:2 W and D plus OL witnesses (c, e, ff²) stand together in supporting ἐξελθόντων αὐτῶν. This could not be a harmonization with parallel accounts in the other Synoptics. The plural reading obviously agrees with the plural ἦλθον εἰς τὸ πέραν which opens the account. Aside from W the supporting witnesses are all Western.

There is an agreement in word order in the last part of Mark 5:2 where D, W, Θ, 565, OL MSS (b, c, e, f, i, q), Arm, Goth, and others of a generally Western nature support ἄνθρωπος ἐκ τῶν μνημείων. Even though this reading is supported by Θ and 565 also, it is, if the property of any text-type, a Western reading.

Again, in 5:3 a variant in word order is supported by D, W, 565, and other Westerns (OL MSS a, b, c, e):

D, W, 565	εἶχεν τὴν κατοίκησιν
TR, A, ℵ, B, Θ, Fam 13	τὴν κατοίκησιν εἶχεν

Other agreements of a less important nature, supported by W and D (plus 565), are συντεριφέναι for συντετρίφθαι in 5:4 (also OL ff², and 1, 28, 131, 209, 251), and μνημείοις for μνήμασιν in Mark 5:5. These slight changes in voice or spelling do not by themselves demonstrate a special textual relationship.

After Mark 5:6 there are very few significant agreements of W with D, and over the whole of Mark 5 and the rest of the Gospel, the quantitative agreement of W with D is considerably less than in Mark 1–4.

If a point is to be specified in the Markan text where W noticeably shifts from comparatively clear Western affiliation, then such a break would be at about Mark 5:6.

In Mark 5 the quantitative relationship of W with D (27.4%) is weaker than the agreement of W with Fam 13 (48.8%), with A (47.6%), B (45.2%), or TR (42.9%). This supports the above contention that Western agreements predominate in the Markan text of W no further than the very early part of Mark 5.

Mark 6 – 16

In Mark 6 W sides more clearly with Fam 13 and Byzantine witnesses than it does with D. Significant agreements of W with D (and 565) consist of two omissions.

> Mark 6:27—omit ὁ βασιλεύς
> Mark 6:33—omit καὶ προῆλθον αὐτούς

In addition, two agreements of W with D are supported also by Θ and 565.

> Mark 6:48—omit πρὸς αὐτούς
> Mark 6:53—omit καὶ προσωρμίσθησαν
> (also Fam 13)

These indicate that Western agreements do not disappear from W after Mark 5 but they do become less frequent.

For the rest of Mark the quantitative relationship of W with D is never again noteworthy. Here follow the relationships of W and of D for each chapter of Mark 6–16.

Ch. 6

W-13	=	61.8%		D-565	=	60.5%
W-TR	=	53.9%		D-TR	=	42.8%
W-A	=	51.3%		D-Θ	=	42.1%
W-B	=	42.8%		D-A	=	39.5%
W-Θ	=	41.4%		D-13	=	35.5%
W-565	=	37.5%		D-W	=	34.2%
W-ℵ	=	36.8%		D-B	=	33.6%
W-D	=	34.2%		D-ℵ	=	25.7%

Ch. 7

W-13	=	59.7%		D-Θ	=	63.6%
W-D	=	50.6%		D-565	=	55.8%
W-TR	=	50.6%		D-W	=	50.6%
W-565	=	49.4%		D-13	=	49.4%
W-Θ	=	48.1%		D-B	=	42.9%
W-A	=	46.8%		D-TR	=	42.9%
W-ℵ	=	42.9%		D-A	=	37.7%
W-B	=	33.8%		D-ℵ	=	33.8%

Ch. 8

W-13	=	61.0%	D-Θ	=	51.0%
W-Θ	=	41.0%	D-565	=	50.0%
W-565	=	40.0%	D-W	=	39.0%
W-D	=	39.0%	D-B	=	35.0%
W-A	=	38.0%	D-A	=	35.0%
W-TR	=	34.0%	D-א	=	34.0%
W-א	=	32.0%	D-TR	=	32.0%
W-B	=	29.0%	D-13	=	32.0%

Ch. 9

W-13	=	53.4%	D-א	=	49.6%
W-B	=	39.7%	D-B	=	45.0%
W-565	=	39.7%	D-A	=	42.7%
W-א	=	38.2%	D-Θ	=	42.0%
W-Θ	=	35.1%	D-TR	=	42.0%
W-D	=	31.3%	D-565	=	37.4%
W-TR	=	31.3%	D-13	=	32.1%
W-A	=	31.3%	D-W	=	31.3%

Ch. 10

W-13	=	61.2%	D-565	=	46.6%
W-A	=	47.6%	D-Θ	=	42.7%
W-D	=	42.7%	D-W	=	42.7%
W-565	=	40.8%	D-TR	=	37.9%
W-Θ	=	36.9%	D-13	=	36.9%
W-TR	=	39.8%	D-A	=	35.0%
W-B	=	30.1%	D-B	=	33.0%
W-א	=	27.2%	D-א	=	32.0%

Ch. 11

W-13	=	51.8%	D-565	=	51.8%
W-565	=	44.7%	D-Θ	=	47.1%
W-B	=	43.5%	D-W	=	36.5%
W-א	=	43.5%	D-13	=	36.5%
W-TR	=	42.4%	D-A	=	34.1%
W-Θ	=	41.2%	D-TR	=	34.1%
W-A	=	40.0%	D-א	=	28.2%
W-D	=	36.5%	D-B	=	22.4%

Ch. 12

W-13	=	54.4%	D-565	=	51.5%
W-Θ	=	44.7%	D-Θ	=	41.7%
W-565	=	40.8%	D-A	=	35.0%
W-TR	=	40.8%	D-B	=	31.1%
W-א	=	37.9%	D-TR	=	31.1%
W-A	=	35.9%	D-א	=	28.2%
W-B	=	35.9%	D-W	=	25.2%
W-D	=	25.2%	D-13	=	25.2%

Ch. 13

W-13	=	54.4%		D-565	=	50.0%
W-TR	=	47.1%		D-Θ	=	39.7%
W-A	=	42.6%		D-B	=	35.3%
W-B	=	42.6%		D-TR	=	32.4%
W-ℵ	=	41.2%		D-W	=	32.4%
W-565	=	41.2%		D-ℵ	=	32.4%
W-Θ	=	35.3%		D-A	=	30.9%
W-D	=	32.4%		D-13	=	25.0%

Ch. 14

W-13	=	65.1%		D-565	=	49.7%
W-A	=	45.0%		D-Θ	=	47.7%
W-TR	=	42.3%		D-ℵ	=	34.9%
W-565	=	40.3%		D-B	=	34.2%
W-B	=	38.9%		D-TR	=	32.2%
W-ℵ	=	36.9%		D-13	=	30.2%
W-Θ	=	34.2%		D-W	=	29.5%
W-D	=	29.5%		D-A	=	29.5%

Chs. 15:1–16:8

W-13	=	57.7%		D-Θ	=	60.6%
W-Θ	=	39.4%		D-565	=	57.7%
W-A	=	39.4%		D-B	=	39.4%
W-D	=	37.0%		D-W	=	38.0%
W-TR	=	36.6%		D-13	=	32.4%
W-B	=	36.6%		D-ℵ	=	31.0%
W-ℵ	=	32.4%		D-TR	=	31.0%
W-565	=	32.4%		D-A	=	31.0%

A chapter by chapter comparison of the data given above will show that, although W and D are sometimes each other's closest allies in the first few chapters of Mark (2, 3, 4), in the rest of Mark their agreement is always conspicuously less than the agreement of either of them with other witnesses.

In this later portion of Mark (6:1–16:8), wherever W does agree with D, the reading is often supported by the Neutral witnesses also. This makes it questionable whether such a reading should be labeled a Western agreement. It is more probable that in these cases the agreement of W and D is simply a joint witness to an old reading with good claims to be original.

In many other cases the agreement of W with D is also supported by Θ, 565, and Fam 13. Since Θ, 565, and Fam 13 are commonly grouped together with W as witnesses to the so-called Caesarean text, are these readings "Caesarean" readings supported by D also? These agreements will be treated in greater detail in the next chapter; it may be said here, however, that it is likely that such agreements of W and other "Caesarean" MSS with D mean that the Caesareans as a whole have some noticeable Western readings. Thus, in Mark 6–16, W is not to be classified as a Western witness. W does, however, show agreements with D that reveal that it may not have escaped here entirely from Western textual influence.

21

SUMMARY AND REFLECTIONS

In Mark 1:1–5:6 Codex W shows an interesting alliance with D and the Western text. Yet it should be remembered that this alliance is not strong enough to justify classing W as a primary Western witness. The strongest agreement of W and D, 57.9 percent in Mark 4, is far below the 70 percent level of agreement suggested as a criterion of a text-type. It seems correct, therefore, to say that in Mark 1:1–5:6, while W has a text that leans more toward the Western textual tradition than toward any other group, this Western affinity in W should not be overemphasized. That is, W shows Western textual influence but in a somewhat muted form.

In Mark 5:7–16:8 W continues to show some trace of Western influence, but W's relationship with D is not the closest for either of them here and W has far fewer agreements with D against the other MSS. Western readings in W's text of Mark 5:7–16:8 appear, but they are significantly fewer than the many Western readings in W's text of Mark 1:1–5:6.

The perplexing problems are: (1) Why is there a pronounced shift in textual affinity in W's text of Mark after 5:6? and (2) How is it that a MS apparently written in Egypt less than a century after the making of Codices B and ℵ (the Neutral MSS) has such agreement with D at all? The "Western" order of the Gospels in Codex W (Matthew, John, Luke, Mark—as found, e.g., in D) shows that W has a clear affinity with Western MSS. It is not, however, the purpose of this study to deal with the question of how W came to have such Western agreement. It is sufficient to say that Codex W shows a text of Mark in Egypt significantly different from the kind of text shown in Codex B. Further, the substantial number of "Western" readings in Codex W shows perhaps a substantial amount of travel and interchange among the Christian groups at the time of W's production. It does not seem possible or especially productive at this time to speculate on exactly how this particular MS acquired these Western readings.

Of the two questions mentioned above, the first is the more intriguing. But there are no indications of how and why the Markan text of W makes this shift in affinity, with Mark 1:1–5:6 being mainly Western, and the rest of Mark much less so. The question is all the more puzzling when it is noted that W has similar shifts in textual affinity in portions other than Mark.[7] Also, it can be pointed out that another important Egyptian MS, Codex Sinaiticus (ℵ), has been found to have similar shifts in textual affinities, and in the first part of the Gospel of John shows striking Western agreements.[8]

In discussing the Western affinities in W, one cannot forget that W is an Egyptian MS, and the question naturally arises as to whether the Neutral text or the kind of text in W is the earliest Egyptian text-type. Is it true, as Colwell seems to suggest, that W represents the old Egyptian text of Mark and that Codex B represents a later "made" text?[9] It must be said against Colwell's view that there

---

[7]W is usually regarded as Byzantine in Matthew and Luke 8:13–24:53. In Luke 1:1–8:12 and John 5:12–21:25 it is Alexandrian. John 1:1–5:11 is a "mixed" text with some Alexandrian and some Western readings (cf. B. M. Metzger, *The Text of the New Testament* 57).

[8]G. D. Fee, "Codex Sinaiticus in the Gospel of John," 23-44.

[9]Colwell, *Studies in Methodology* 54.

is very little evidence for a recensional activity in Egypt that led to the making of the kind of text found in Codex B.[10] The discovery of P^{75} and P^{66} shows that the Neutral tradition can be traced back to the earliest of the textual witnesses.[11] Fee has shown that the "recensional" activity reflected in the corrections in P^{66} in John is not a "scholarly" activity "of a kind that produces the Neutral text-type, but rather of a kind that culminates at a later date in the process of textual transmission called the Byzantine text-type."[12] Our final chapter shows that the readings distinctive to W are ones that do not have good claims to being authentically Markan. As will be noted in the later chapter dealing with P^{45}, there is a good chance that W and P^{45} represent a text of Mark that once may have been more closely related to the Neutral text-type, but was later edited and reworded with the interests of popular readers in mind. The suggestion of the present writer is that W represents a "corrupted" Egyptian text of Mark, this "corruption" coming in part from the influence of the Western readings. Further, and very importantly, this Western "corruption" in W seems to explain partly the relationship of W with Θ and 565. It is to the important question of the relationship of W with these Caesareans that we now must turn.

---

[10]All theories about "Alexandrian scribes" and their interests and abilities in recreating more original readings seem to this writer to be as poorly supported by evidence as Bousset's once popular, but now discredited theory of a "Hesychian" recension being responsible for the Neutral text. See Frederick G. Kenyon, "Hesychius and the Text of the New Testament," *Mémorial Lagrange* (1940) 245-50. Hedley seems to have favored some such view as that described above in which the Neutral MSS are seen as bearers of authentic textual tradition rather than as works resulting from some recensional activity ("The Egyptian Texts of the Gospels and Acts," 225-26). Hedley attributed views of the Neutral text as a recensional text to the "nonsense talked about Hesychius by Bousset, von Soden, and their followers" (226 n. 37). Now see G. D. Fee, "P^{75}, P^{66}, and Origen: The Myth of Early Textual Recension in Alexandria," *New Dimensions in New Testament Study* (ed. R. N. Longenecker and M. C. Tenney; Grand Rapids: Zondervan, 1974) 19-45.

[11]On P^{75} see C. L. Porter, "Papyrus Bodmer XV (P^{75}) and the Text of Codex Vaticanus," *JBL* 81(1962) 363-76; G. D. Fee, "Codex Sinaiticus in the Gospel of John," and on P^{66} see Fee, *Papyrus Bodmer II (P^{66}): Its Textual Relationships and Scribal Characteristics* (SD 34, 1968).

[12]Fee, *Papyrus Bodmer II* 82-83.

CHAPTER III

CODEX W AND THE CAESAREAN TEXT

THE PROBLEM

Streeter placed W among the witnesses to the Caesarean text-type in Mark 5:31–16:8, and, indeed, he ranked W as one of the best witnesses to this text-type, hailing W as proof that a single text lay behind the readings attested in the Caesarean MSS.[1] As noted in the first chapter of this study, further reflection by other scholars led to a somewhat modified estimate of W's relationship to the Caesarean text, and most scholars have accepted now the view made popular by Ayuso and the Lakes. This view places W with other MSS (mainly P[45] and Fam 13) as leading witnesses to a "pre-Caesarean" text that is the early form of a text represented by Θ, 565, and 700, the "Caesarean" text proper. The term "pre-Caesarean" bares the implicit view that W has a special relationship to the later Caesarean MSS. Some have objected to this description of the relationship of W with Θ and the other later MSS. The question, then, is to what degree W is actually related to the later form of the Caesarean text.

THIS STUDY

In this study, Codex Θ and 565 were used as the representatives of the later Caesarean text proper. These two are usually ranked as the leading witnesses to this text-type.[2] The proponents of the Caesarean text always stated that no one MS gave the text of the archetype. But, comparatively speaking, it does seem legitimate to say that Θ is perhaps the best single representative of the theoretical later text. For purposes of quantitative measurement, therefore, Θ may be taken as a primary Caesarean witness, and the quantitative agreement of W with Θ will represent accurately the agreement with the theoretical later Caesarean text.

This chapter will show that Codex W is not a Caesarean MS—not even a "pre-Caesarean" MS. The quantitative relationship of W with Codex Θ and with 565 shows no special textual relationship. Further, the specific agreements of W with Θ will be examined to reinforce this point. It will be shown that what agreements there are between W and Θ do not demand a genetic relationship between these two MSS to account for these agreements. We shall notice that the agreements

---

[1] "The Washington MS and the Caesarean Text of the Gospels," *JTS* 27(1925/26) 144; *idem*, "The Washington MS of the Gospels," *HTR* 19(1926) 165-72.

[2] K. Lake stated that Θ had a smaller "admixture" of Byzantine readings than any other MS of the Caesarean group ("The Text of the Gospels and the Koridethi Codex," *HTR* 16[1923] 275-77). See also Lake, Blake, New, "The Caesarean Text of Mark," 253-57, where in Lake's view Θ is equalled in value only by 565 for reconstructing the text of the theoretical archetype.

of W and Θ can be explained almost entirely as "Western" readings shared by these two witnesses and/or as coincidental agreements in common kinds of scribal corruptions of the text of Mark.[3]

EXCURSUS

Before presenting the data that reveal the relationship of W and Θ, it will be helpful to point out something that will aid in following the discussion at many points. The Gospel of Mark, whatever its authorship, is distinctive in comparison with the other Synoptics, for while there is a basic similarity of content and arrangement among the first three Gospels, Mark's style of writing is somewhat peculiar. The use of expressions that may be described as awkward or rustic cause the Gospel of Mark to appear somewhat unlettered or even crude.[4] If, as it appears to most scholars, the writers of Matthew and Luke used Mark as a source, it appears also that they generally changed these peculiarities and crudities, both of them often making the same improvement. Perhaps because of the fuller accounts of the story of Jesus and his teachings contained in them, it appears that Matthew and Luke were far more widely read and used for liturgical purposes. This means that, in the mind of anyone accustomed to hearing the Gospels as they were read in church, the form of the Matthean and Lukan accounts would be more familiar.

These two things—the less literary Markan style and the scribes' greater familiarity with the other Synoptic Gospels—prompted a great deal of scribal improvement, correction, and supplementation of Mark as it was copied. Now it will be insisted repeatedly in the following pages that, where a variant is a harmonization to the other Synoptic accounts or where the variant is an improvement of Markan style to accord with more widely accepted Hellenistic tastes, agreements in these kinds of variants are not very significant as indications of genetic relationship. It should be obvious that while such changes in Mark's text might be similar, if not identical, they often could have been made independently.

The final chapter of this study shows variants supported only by W that are examples of independent scribal corruption of the text. These examples will provide justification for recognizing that independent scribal changes in the direction of common scribal tendencies produced many coincidental agreements. This idea has not been given its due importance and the result has been an overestimating of the importance of individual agreements of MSS.[5]

---

[3]We shall give special attention to the agreements of W and Θ, rather than W and 565 because Θ is usually regarded as the better representative of the Caesarean text. The average quantitative relationship of W and 565 over Mark 6–16 (40.7%) is not appreciably greater than the W-Θ relationship over the same portion of Mark (39.7%), and this slight difference is probably accounted for by the fact that 565 agrees a little more often with D in Mark 6–16 (D-Θ: 47.8%, D-565: 51.1%).

[4]The most complete treatment of Mark's peculiarities is by C. H. Turner, "Marcan Style: Notes, Critical and Exegetical on the Second Gospel," *JTS* 25(1924) 377-86; 26(1925) 12-20, 145-56, 225-40, 337-46; 27(1926) 58-62; 28(1927) 9-30, 349-62; 29(1928) 275-89, 346-61. Turner shows how often Matthew and Luke have the same correction of Mark independently. Shorter accounts can be found in most good commentaries; e.g., Henry Barclay Swete, *The Gospel According to St. Mark* (3rd ed.; London: Macmillan & Co., 1908) xxxviii-xliv; Vincent Taylor, *The Gospel According to St. Mark* (2nd ed.; London: Macmillan & Co., 1966) 44-54; C. E. B. Cranfield, *The Gospel According to Saint Mark* (Cambridge: Cambridge University Press, 1966) 20-21. Most recently, see E. J. Pryke, *Redactional Style in the Marcan Gospel* (SNTSMS 33; Cambridge: Cambridge University, 1978).

[5]See E. C. Colwell, *Studies in Methodology* 106-7. Colwell is a pioneer in demonstrating the position argued for in this study.

Mark 1–5

In the early chapters of Mark (1–5) W appears to have no clearly distinctive relationship with Θ or with 565. It should be remembered that W shows itself to be more Western here than in any part of Mark. The relationships of W, Θ, and 565 are set forth here.

Ch. 1

W-TR	= 48.9%	Θ-565	= 54.5%	565-13	= 69.3%
W-D	= 44.3%	Θ-D	= 48.7%	565-Θ	= 54.5%
W-Θ	= 43.2%	Θ-TR	= 46.6%	565-TR	= 45.5%
W-A	= 43.2%	Θ-13	= 45.5%	565-A	= 44.3%
W-565	= 34.1%	Θ-A	= 45.5%	565-ℵ	= 42.1%
W-13	= 33.0%	Θ-W	= 43.2%	565-B	= 37.5%
W-B	= 38.6%	Θ-B	= 43.2%	565-D	= 35.2%
W-ℵ	= 30.7%	Θ-ℵ	= 40.9%	565-W	= 34.1%

Ch. 2

W-D	= 46.8%	Θ-565	= 55.1%	565-13	= 62.3%
W-ℵ	= 34.8%	Θ-B	= 53.6%	565-Θ	= 55.1%
W-B	= 30.4%	Θ-ℵ	= 47.8%	565-TR	= 55.1%
W-A	= 27.5%	Θ-13	= 39.1%	565-ℵ	= 55.1%
W-Θ	= 26.1%	Θ-A	= 37.7%	565-A	= 53.6%
W-TR	= 26.1%	Θ-TR	= 36.2%	565-B	= 46.4%
W-565	= 24.6%	Θ-D	= 36.2%	565-D	= 36.2%
W-13	= 23.2%	Θ-W	= 26.1%	565-W	= 24.6%

Ch. 3

W-D	= 46.9%	Θ-565	= 64.1%	565-Θ	= 64.1%
W-Θ	= 28.1%	Θ-13	= 51.6%	565-B	= 57.8%
W-13	= 28.1%	Θ-ℵ	= 46.9%	565-A	= 54.7%
W-ℵ	= 28.1%	Θ-B	= 43.8%	565-13	= 51.6%
W-B	= 28.1%	Θ-A	= 43.8%	565-TR	= 48.4%
W-565	= 25.0%	Θ-TR	= 37.5%	565-ℵ	= 45.3%
W-A	= 23.4%	Θ-D	= 32.8%	565-D	= 29.7%
W-TR	= 23.4%	Θ-W	= 28.1%	565-W	= 25.0%

Ch. 4

W-D	= 57.9%	Θ-565	= 76.8%	565-Θ	= 76.8%
W-Θ	= 42.1%	Θ-13	= 47.4%	565-13	= 55.8%
W-13	= 35.8%	Θ-D	= 46.3%	565-D	= 53.7%
W-565	= 34.7%	Θ-W	= 42.1%	565-TR	= 41.1%
W-B	= 27.4%	Θ-TR	= 38.9%	565-A	= 41.1%
W-A	= 26.3%	Θ-A	= 36.8%	565-ℵ	= 36.8%
W-ℵ	= 25.3%	Θ-ℵ	= 35.8%	565-W	= 34.7%
W-TR	= 23.2%	Θ-B	= 34.7%	565-B	= 31.6%

Ch. 5

W-13	= 48.8%	Θ-565	= 53.6%	565-D	= 63.1%
W-A	= 47.6%	Θ-13	= 48.8%	565-Θ	= 53.6%

W-B	=	45.2%	Θ-א	=	46.4%	565-TR	=	46.4%
W-א	=	42.9%	Θ-B	=	46.4%	565-13	=	36.9%
W-TR	=	42.9%	Θ-TR	=	41.7%	565-W	=	36.9%
W-565	=	36.9%	Θ-A	=	41.7%	565-א	=	34.5%
W-Θ	=	33.3%	Θ-D	=	40.5%	565-A	=	31.0%
W-D	=	27.4%	Θ-W	=	33.3%	565-B	=	27.4%

In Mark 1 the relationship of W with Θ (43.2%) is almost as strong as any other relationship of W but is not exceptional. In Mark 2–3 W and Θ clearly cannot be classified together, since their quantitative relationship is quite low—26.1 percent in Mark 2, 28.1 percent in Mark 3. In Mark 4 their relationship is stronger again (42.1%). Still, for both W and Θ, this figure is exceeded by figures representing textual relationships of W or Θ with other MSS. In Mark 5 the figure drops again (33.3%). The W-565 relationship in Mark 1–5 is even weaker. Over the whole of Mark 1–5, then, it is apparent that W is not a Caesarean witness.

As mentioned, W and Θ do approach each other somewhat in Mark 4, whereas in the chapters immediately preceding and following their quantitative relationship with each other is very weak. Let us note what accounts for this relatively closer agreement in Mark 4.

It will be helpful to note the major supporters, from among the control MSS, of the forty agreements of W with Θ in this chapter.

> TR supports W-Θ = 12
> A supports W-Θ = 11
> B supports W-Θ = 12
> א supports W-Θ = 13
> D supports W-Θ = 30
> D the lone uncial supporter = 14

That is, in thirty out of forty cases, D is among the supporters. In fourteen cases it is the only uncial support. Further, a glance at the tables above will show that in Mark 4 both W and Θ are closer to D than in chs. 2, 3, and 5. The conclusion seems inescapable that W and Θ agree more closely in Mark 4 precisely because there they both have a noticeable number of Western agreements. Therefore, the factor common to W and Θ here is basically "Western" readings, and W and Θ do not show any special relationship in these chapters.

Mark 6 – 16

We shall now discuss Mark 6:1–16:8, where W is supposedly a Caesarean witness. Here are the quantitative relationships of W, Θ, and 565 with each control MS.

Ch. 6

W-13	=	61.8%	Θ-565	=	55.9%	565-D	=	60.5%
W-TR	=	53.9%	Θ-א	=	44.7%	565-Θ	=	55.9%
W-A	=	51.3%	Θ-13	=	44.1%	565-TR	=	41.4%
W-B	=	42.8%	Θ-B	=	43.4%	565-A	=	40.1%
W-Θ	=	41.4%	Θ-D	=	42.1%	565-13	=	40.1%
W-565	=	37.5%	Θ-W	=	41.4%	565-W	=	37.5%

W-ℵ   = 36.8%   Θ-TR = 41.4%   565-ℵ   = 25.7%
W-D   = 34.2%   Θ-A   = 40.1%   565-B   = 23.7%

Ch. 7
W-13 = 59.7%   Θ-565 = 70.1%   565-Θ   = 70.1%
W-D   = 50.6%   Θ-D   = 63.6%   565-D   = 55.8%
W-TR = 50.6%   Θ-B   = 49.4%   565-TR = 51.9%
W-565 = 49.4%   Θ-W   = 48.1%   565-W   = 49.4%
W-Θ   = 48.1%   Θ-ℵ   = 44.2%   565-13 = 48.1%
W-A   = 46.8%   Θ-13 = 44.2%   565-A   = 48.1%
W-ℵ   = 42.9%   Θ-TR = 41.6%   565-B   = 37.7%
W-B   = 33.8%   Θ-A   = 36.4%   565-ℵ   = 29.9%

Ch. 8
W-13 = 61.0%   Θ-565 = 78.0%   565-Θ   = 78.0%
W-Θ   = 41.0%   Θ-D   = 51.0%   565-D   = 50.0%
W-565 = 40.0%   Θ-A   = 43.0%   565-A   = 44.0%
W-D   = 39.0%   Θ-13 = 43.0%   565-W   = 40.0%
W-A   = 38.0%   Θ-W   = 41.0%   565-TR = 39.0%
W-TR = 34.0%   Θ-TR = 41.0%   565-13 = 38.0%
W-ℵ   = 32.0%   Θ-B   = 33.0%   565-B   = 36.0%
W-B   = 29.0%   Θ-ℵ   = 33.0%   565-ℵ   = 35.0%

Ch. 9
W-13 = 53.4%   Θ-565 = 64.1%   565-Θ   = 64.1%
W-565 = 39.7%   Θ-13 = 46.6%   565-13 = 48.9%
W-B   = 39.7%   Θ-D   = 42.0%   565-TR = 43.5%
W-ℵ   = 38.2%   Θ-B   = 43.5%   565-ℵ   = 42.7%
W-Θ   = 35.1%   Θ-ℵ   = 43.5%   565-A   = 41.2%
W-D   = 31.3%   Θ-TR = 41.2%   565-B   = 40.5%
W-TR = 31.3%   Θ-A   = 37.4%   565-W   = 39.7%
W-A   = 31.3%   Θ-W   = 35.1%   565-D   = 37.4%

Ch. 10
W-13 = 61.2%   Θ-565 = 74.8%   565-Θ   = 74.8%
W-A   = 47.6%   Θ-D   = 42.7%   565-D   = 46.6%
W-D   = 42.7%   Θ-13 = 38.8%   565-13 = 46.6%
W-565 = 40.8%   Θ-W   = 36.9%   565-W   = 40.8%
W-TR = 39.8%   Θ-ℵ   = 34.0%   565-A   = 39.8%
W-Θ   = 36.9%   Θ-B   = 31.1%   565-TR = 35.9%
W-B   = 30.1%   Θ-A   = 28.2%   565-ℵ   = 34.0%
W-ℵ   = 27.2%   Θ-TR = 26.2%   565-B   = 25.2%

Ch. 11
W-13 = 51.8%   Θ-565 = 67.1%   565-Θ   = 67.1%
W-565 = 44.7%   Θ-D   = 47.1%   565-D   = 51.8%
W-ℵ   = 43.5%   Θ-13 = 44.7%   565-13 = 44.7%
W-B   = 43.5%   Θ-W   = 41.2%   565-W   = 44.7%
W-TR = 42.4%   Θ-TR = 41.2%   565-TR = 41.2%
W-Θ   = 41.2%   Θ-A   = 38.8%   565-A   = 35.3%

W-A	=	40.0%	Θ-B	=	34.1%	565-B	=	30.6%
W-D	=	36.5%	Θ-א	=	31.8%	565-א	=	29.4%

Ch. 12

W-13	=	54.4%	Θ-565	=	76.7%	565-Θ	=	76.7%
W-Θ	=	44.7%	Θ-13	=	46.6%	565-D	=	51.5%
W-565	=	40.8%	Θ-W	=	44.7%	565-13	=	42.7%
W-TR	=	40.8%	Θ-D	=	41.7%	565-W	=	40.8%
W-א	=	37.9%	Θ-א	=	38.8%	565-TR	=	39.8%
W-A	=	35.9%	Θ-TR	=	37.9%	565-א	=	37.9%
W-B	=	35.9%	Θ-B	=	36.9%	565-A	=	35.9%
W-D	=	25.2%	Θ-A	=	35.0%	565-B	=	29.1%

Ch. 13

W-13	=	54.4%	Θ-565	=	76.5%	565-Θ	=	76.5%
W-TR	=	47.1%	Θ-13	=	58.8%	565-13	=	54.4%
W-A	=	42.6%	Θ-D	=	39.7%	565-D	=	50.0%
W-B	=	42.6%	Θ-TR	=	35.3%	565-W	=	41.2%
W-565	=	41.2%	Θ-W	=	35.3%	565-TR	=	36.8%
W-א	=	41.2%	Θ-A	=	33.8%	565-A	=	35.3%
W-Θ	=	35.4%	Θ-א	=	29.4%	565-א	=	27.9%
W-D	=	32.4%	Θ-B	=	19.1%	565-B	=	26.5%

Ch. 14

W-13	=	65.1%	Θ-565	=	75.2%	565-Θ	=	75.2%
W-A	=	45.0%	Θ-D	=	47.7%	565-D	=	49.7%
W-TR	=	42.3%	Θ-13	=	47.0%	565-13	=	47.0%
W-565	=	40.3%	Θ-TR	=	38.3%	565-W	=	40.3%
W-B	=	38.9%	Θ-A	=	36.9%	565-A	=	33.6%
W-א	=	36.9%	Θ-B	=	34.9%	565-TR	=	32.2%
W-Θ	=	34.2%	Θ-W	=	34.2%	565-א	=	27.5%
W-D	=	29.5%	Θ-א	=	31.5%	565-B	=	26.8%

Chs. 15–16

W-13	=	57.7%	Θ-565	=	80.3%	565-Θ	=	80.3%
W-Θ	=	39.4%	Θ-D	=	60.6%	565-D	=	57.7%
W-A	=	39.4%	Θ-W	=	39.4%	565-13	=	33.8%
W-D	=	38.0%	Θ-13	=	39.4%	565-W	=	32.4%
W-TR	=	36.6%	Θ-TR	=	32.4%	565-א	=	25.4%
W-B	=	36.6%	Θ-א	=	31.0%	565-TR	=	23.9%
W-א	=	32.4%	Θ-B	=	29.6%	565-A	=	22.5%
W-565	=	32.4%	Θ-A	=	28.2%	565-B	=	22.5%

In Mark 6 W and Θ are unimpressive in their agreement (41.4%). A glance at the tables will show that in Mark 6, as in Mark 5, W moves away from any close affiliation with D (34.2% in Mark 6). It seems that both W and Θ must be fairly close to D before they show any noticeable affiliation with each other.

In Mark 7 both W and Θ are more closely allied with D. D and Θ agree 63.6 percent, and D and W agree 50.6 percent. As one might expect, W and Θ also reach a closer accord with each other here (48.1%). An examination of their agreements in this chapter shows that D supports 26 of their 37 agreements. In 5 cases D is the only supporting uncial from among the control MSS. W and Θ (plus 565) agree against all the other control MSS at only one place. The major variants here (Mark 7:35) are as follows:

A, TR, Fam 13   εὐθέως διηνοίχθησαν
ℵ, B, D   ἠνύγησαν
W, 565, Θ   εὐθέως διηνύγησαν

This is very slim evidence upon which to build a case for some special relationship of W with Θ and 565. One must remember that a few distinctive agreements are not enough to demonstrate a truly distinctive relationship between MSS. There must be an overall, large quantitative agreement including numerous distinctive readings.[6] This caution has been ignored often in past work, but it will not do to repeat those mistakes again.[7]

The table for Mark 8 shows that W and Θ have a weaker relationship (41.0%) there. Also, each has a weaker relationship with D in this chapter. An examination of the points of agreement shows that in eight out of the forty-one agreements of W with Θ, D is the only uncial supporter among the control MSS. W and Θ receive no such strong support from any of the other textual representatives. The support of D appears (with or without other witnesses) in twenty-seven out of forty-one agreements, far more frequently than any other control MS. (Codex A is next in frequency of support, at seventeen places.)

W and Θ agree against the "non-Caesarean" control MSS seven times. In comparison, note that ℵ and B agree against all other control MSS eleven times. It will be helpful to look at these special agreements of W with Θ to see what they tell about the textual element common to these two witnesses.

In 8:2 W and Θ have ἐπὶ τῷ ὄχλῳ where other control witnesses have the accusative or genitive form. This agreement of W and Θ is not significant in that the preposition ἐπί is used with all these cases, often interchangeably.[8] The preference for the dative form attests only a common stylistic tendency. It does not evidence a special relationship of W with Θ.

In 8:35 the phrase τὴν ψυχὴν αὐτοῦ occurs twice in the TR. W and Θ, with Fam 13, agree with TR in the first case but in the second case read τὴν ἑαυτοῦ ψυχήν. Codex B has τὴν ψυχὴν αὐτοῦ in the second occurrence of the phrase, but in the first occurrence reads τὴν ἑαυτοῦ ψυχήν. The variants in B and the "Caesareans" are basically the same but not at the same point in the passage. The fact that B and the Caesarean MSS have the same alternative for the repetition of the phrase τὴν ψυχὴν αὐτοῦ shows that the agreement of W with Θ here is not

---

[6]It will be noticed that W, 565, and Θ here prefer a compound verb over the simple form attested by the impressive agreement of ℵ, B, and D. Hort mentioned the substitution of compound verb forms for simple ones as a characteristic of the Western witnesses. Is this reading of W and Θ only another Western reading which was modified into a passive voice and accepted into the Byzantine witnesses? See B. F. Westcott and F. J. A. Hort, *The New Testament in the Original Greek: Introduction* (London: Macmillan, 1882) 123-24.

[7]See E. C. Colwell, *Studies in Methodology* 10-11, 28. Note also Frederik Wisse and Paul R. McReynolds, "Family E and the Profile Method," *Bib* 51(1970) 67-75.

[8]BDF §§ 233-35.

really very distinctive, and does not demonstrate a special relationship of W with Θ.

The W-Θ agreement at Mark 8:14 differs from the Neutral-Byzantine reading by omitting the phrase καὶ εἰ μή, an omission supported by Fam 13 and 565. However, in the next phrase the witnesses divide as follows:

TR, A, ℵ, B	ἕνα ἄρτον οὐκ εἶχον
P⁴⁵, Θ, 565	ἕνα μόνον ἄρτον ἔχοντες
W, Fam 13	ἕνα μόνον ἔχοντες ἄρτον
D	ἕνα ἄρτον εἶχον

The full sentence, as it appears in the Neutral-Byzantine witnesses, apparently seemed awkward, and all the other variants appear to be attempts to smooth out the syntax. The agreement of W, Θ, 565, and Fam 13 in the omission of καὶ εἰ μή is interesting, but is an improvement in the sentence that could have occurred in the minds of scribes independently.

In 8:7 W and Θ agree once more against the control witnesses. The major variants at this point are:

A, TR, Fam 13	παραθεῖναι καὶ αὐτά
B	καὶ ταῦτα παρατιθέναι
D	καὶ αὐτοὺς ἐκέλευσεν παρατειθέναι
W, Θ	παραθεῖναι

The interesting thing here is that the phrasing in D appears to be a singular reading. It is the reading supported by W and Θ that apparently lies behind the OL and Vg;[9] and it seems that D here leaves the Western tradition and that W and Θ are truer to the Western reading! This W-Θ agreement is, then, hardly evidence of a "Caesarean" text.

In 8:29 W and Θ, with Fam 1, Fam 13, 28, and some Syr MSS, omit καὶ αὐτός. This is more an example of the somewhat free treatment accorded to pronouns in the textual transmission of the NT than it is good evidence of genetic relationship.

A reading in which W and Θ agree against the non-Caesareans in Mark 8:15 gives τῶν Ἡρωδιάνων for Ἡρῴδου. This variant is also supported by Fam 1, Fam 13, P⁴⁵, 565, the OL MSS i and k, and the Sah, Geo, and Arm. Is this a Caesarean reading or is it better described as an editorial correction with widely distributed support? The reading of W and Θ and the others is no doubt a scribal attempt to "straighten out" the alternative reading. The Herodians are mentioned in the Gospels as enemies of Christ and are connected with the Pharisees in Mark as the ones who laid plans to arrest Jesus (Mark 3:6). Herod is not linked with the Pharisees and so reference to him here must have seemed out of place. For that reason the reference to Herod and not to the Herodians is more likely original. If the reading of W and Θ were original it is doubtful that the reference

---

[9]In this study the apparatus of Legg's work on Mark has been relied upon heavily in detecting the support from among manuscripts not included in the list of control manuscripts and for support by the versions. S. C. E. Legg, *Novum Testamentum Graece: Euangelium secundum Marcum* (Oxford: Clarendon Press, 1935). This work has been checked by use of Constantinus Tischendorf, *Novum Testamentum graece* (8th ed.; Leipzig: J. C. Hinrichs, 1872) I.

to Herod would have been created. Thus, the fact that the reference to the Herodians is an easily explained attempt to "improve" the text, plus the fact that the same improvement occurs in such widely scattered witnesses, make it unlikely that the W-Θ agreement here indicates a special relationship between these two MSS.

The agreement in 8:23 unites W and Θ against the non-Caesarean witnesses in reading αὐτοῦ in place of τοῦ τυφλοῦ. The reading could be described as more concise in that it avoids another use of the noun "blind man," which has already been used in the preceding sentence. This use of the pronoun instead of the noun is also supported by Fam 13, Fam 1, P⁴⁵, 565, and 700. If it is a Caesarean reading, then the Caesarean text favors more concise readings that reveal an editor's hand.

After reviewing these seven agreements of W with Θ against the non-Caesarean control witnesses, one is left with little reason to believe that W and Θ have a special relationship. Two readings are inconsequential stylistic variants (8:2, 35). One more agreement is best labeled "Western" because of the similarity to readings in many Western witnesses (8:7). Two more are supported only by "Caesarean" witnesses (8:14, 29) but both the "Caesarean" readings are attempts at concise expression—a scribal tendency—not necessarily evidence of genetic relationship. The remaining agreement appears to be a deliberate change toward an "easier" reading—a change easily explained, and one with scattered support. The W-Θ reading in 8:15 appears to be a "correction" of Mark supported by a crowd of witnesses, the diversity of which brands the reading as valueless in showing genetic relationships.

Mark 9

In Mark 9 both W and Θ are at a somewhat greater distance from D (W-D = 31.3%; Θ-D = 42.0%) and are also less close to each other (W-Θ = 35.1%). This seems to confirm the rule detected earlier in Mark that the relationship of W and Θ with each other is determined by the relationship of each with D. Of the forty-six agreements of W and Θ counted in Mark 9, D is in support eighteen times. TR supports W-Θ eighteen times, and Neutral support from B is present twenty-two times. These figures indicate that in Mark 9 the proportion of W-Θ agreements that can be labeled "Western readings" is less than in Mark 8. It bears repeating that in Mark 9, precisely because of a diminished number of Western readings, the total percentage of agreement between W and Θ is significantly less (Mark 8: W-Θ = 41.0%; Mark 9: W-Θ = 35.1%).

There are eleven agreements of W and Θ against the non-Caesarean MSS. In 9:2 W and Θ add ἐν τῷ προσεύχεσθαι αὐτούς before μετεμορφώθη. This reading is supported by Fam 13, P⁴⁵, and 565 (or to be exact, very similar readings are supported by all these witnesses: Θ and 565 have αὐτόν instead of αὐτούς and 565 has ἐγένετο at the beginning of the phrase). A glance at a Gospel synopsis[10] will show that the additional phrase is a clear harmonization with the parallel in Luke 9:29. Θ and 565 agree more closely with the parallel than do P⁴⁵, W, and Fam 13, and this minor divergence among these "Caesarean" MSS seems to be

[10]The synopsis used for this study was Kurt Aland, ed., *Synopsis Quattuor Evangeliorum* (2nd ed.; Stuttgart: Württembergische Bibelanstalt, 1965).

evidence that the similar reading in the Markan text of all these MSS is due more to similar harmonistic desires than to a strong genealogical relationship. Even if the exact reading were shared by these so-called Caesarean MSS, the fact that it is a clear harmonization reading makes it weak proof of a special relationship. Of all possible kinds of coincidental agreements, harmonizing readings are surely the most likely to be coincidental.

The insertion of ἰδού before ἐγένετο νεφέλη in 9:7 is agreed upon by the main Greek "Caesarean" MSS (W, Θ, Fam 13, 28, 565, 700). Doubtless this reading is also a harmonization of the Markan passage with the parallel in Matt 17:5.[11]

In 9:28 there are two special agreements of W, Θ, 565, and Fam 13 against the other control witnesses, and the first reading is the addition of προσῆλθον αὐτῷ after οἶκον. This too is a harmonization with the Matt 17:19 parallel.

These three cases show that the MSS grouped as Caesareans seem to have a noticeable tendency toward harmonization.[12] This common tendency does not, however, prove common ancestry.

Of the remaining special agreements of W and Θ in Mark 9, four appear to show Western affinity. In 9:11 the substitution of τί οὖν for ὅτι before λέγουσιν seems to be supported by such witnesses as the OL, Vg, and Syr Peshitto. It further seems to be a possible harmonization with the reading in Matt 17:10. The ὅτι interrogative was not favored by the other Synoptics or by scribes.[13]

Again, at 9:21 W, Θ, and 565, with the OL, Vg, and several other witnesses, support ἐξ οὗ rather than ὡς.[14]

In 9:37 W and Θ (with Fam 13) support ἐκ in place of ἕν. This substitution seems to have the support of some important OL MSS (b, c, d, ff, i, q, r¹). In 9:42 the W-Θ variant is the same as that of D and the OL reading, the aorist passive ἐβλήθη against the perfect βέβληται, but with a slightly different word order.

The remaining four agreements of W and Θ against the non-Caesarean witnesses include another agreement in 9:28. There the reading of W and Θ (with Fam 13 and 565) is only a minor variant, giving the aorist form ἐπηρώτησαν where others have the imperfect ἐπηρώτων, and the addition of λέγοντες (also attested by P⁴⁵). This minor variant is typical of the readings that might be considered distinctive Caesarean readings, very small and almost insignificant.[15]

In 9:10 W, Θ, and other Caesarean MSS (Fam 13, 565, 700) read οἱ δέ for καί. This is a variant in the text of Mark that is attested in many MSS at varying

---

[11]Note C. H. Turner's study of the use of ἰδού in the Synoptics, "Marcan Usage," *JTS* 28(1927) 21-22.

[12]E. F. Hills emphasized the harmonistic tendency in the Caesarean MSS ("The Caesarean Family of New Testament Manuscripts," 69-70); see also Lagrange, "Les papyrus Chester Beatty," 10, 18-19, 40-41.

[13]Note C. H. Turner's study of the ὅτι interrogative in Mark as a Markan peculiarity, "Marcan Usage," *JTS* 27(1926) 58-60.

[14]In such cases as this where there may be several variants, references to substitution, omission, or addition mean the reading of W and the MS being discussed *in comparison to the text of Mark given* in the *Synopsis* edited by K. Aland (n. 10 above).

[15]Lagrange noticed this long ago ("Le group dit césaréen," 495).

points, owing to Mark's repetitious use of the καί, and it is therefore of little importance as proof of strong genealogical ties.[16]

At 9:17 W, Θ, and Fam 13 agree in reading εἶπεν αὐτῷ before διδάσκαλε. This is a variation in the formula used here to introduce the quotation. Such variation is common, and Hort mentioned it as especially characteristic of that loosely agreeing group of MSS—the Western text.[17]

In 9:36 W, Θ, and other MSS (Fam 1, 28, 565, Arm) omit αὐτό after ἔστησεν. This is another example of the way some MSS treated pronouns, for the same omission occurs in the Lukan parallel (9:49) in D and the OL MSS. Possibly the reading of the "Caesareans" here in the Markan passage is a harmonization to the Western text of Luke or is simply an example of the "Western" tendency at work in Mark. The agreements of W with Θ in Mark 9 show again that the textual connection of these two MSS is very weak and easily accounted for.

Mark 10

In Mark 10 D and Θ retain about the same percentage of agreement (42.7%) as in the previous chapter of Mark. In this chapter W is noticeably closer to D than in ch. 9 (Mark 9: 31.3%; Mark 10: 42.7%), and, true to pattern, is also slightly closer to Θ than in ch. 9 (Mark 9: 35.1%; Mark 10: 36.9%). D is among the supporters of W and Θ in twenty of their thirty-eight agreements. D stands with these "Caesareans" against the other text traditions six times. The Neutrals are clearly present in twelve agreements and stand with W and Θ against the others only four times. This seems to show again that in the agreements of W and Θ "Western" support is pronounced.

Among the agreements of W and Θ against the non-Caesarean control MSS is the addition of εἰ θέλεις τέλειος εἶναι in Mark 10:21 before ἕν, also supported by Fam 13, 28, 565, 1071, K, N, Y, Π, Σ, the Sah, and the Boh. The reading is a clear harmonization to the Matt 19:21 parallel. The wide array of supporting witnesses shows that it was a popular harmonization, and this fact makes any agreement of MSS on this reading poor evidence of special relationship.

Also, in 10:27 the reading τοῦτο ἀδύνατον for ἀδύνατον, found in numerous witnesses (W, Θ, Fam 13, 28, 700, 1071, Σ, Peshitto and Sinaitic Syr, Arm), is a clear harmonization with the Matt 19:26 parallel reading. It should be noted that a slightly fuller harmonization is supported by D and OL witnesses at the same point (τοῦτο ἀδύνατόν ἐστιν). This is, then, neither an important nor an unusual agreement.

The exact reading of W and Θ in 10:12 is not found in non-Caesarean MSS but is very similar to the readings in D and in ℵ and B. The readings are set out here so that the reader may see the relative insignificance of the W-Θ variant.

ℵ-B	γαμήσῃ ἄλλον
W-Θ, Fam 13, 565	καὶ γαμήσῃ ἄλλον
D	καὶ ἄλλον γαμήσῃ

[16]Margaret E. Thrall states (*Greek Particles in the New Testament* [NTTS 3; Leiden: E. J. Brill, 1962] 65), "There appears to have been an overwhelming tendency for scribes to alter καί to δέ. . . ."

[17]Westcott and Hort, *The New Testament in the Original Greek: Introduction* 123.

34

This is especially insignificant when one notes that W and Θ disagree in the preceding phrase:

W   ἐὰν ἀπολύσῃ γύνη
Θ   γύνη ἐάν ἐξέλθη

The two remaining special agreements of W and Θ in this chapter are both minor and common stylistic improvements: οἱ δέ for καί in 10:2, and παρὰ μέν for παρά in 10:27. From this examination, it is clear that ch. 10 also fails to produce evidence of a strong relationship between W and Θ.

Mark 11

In ch. 11 the quantitative agreement of W and Θ increases slightly to 41.2 percent, but this figure in itself shows a very unremarkable relationship between the two MSS. In eighteen of their thirty-five agreements D joins W and Θ. This shows again the large role of the D-type text in explaining the agreements of W and Θ.

The agreements of W and Θ against the non-Caesarean control MSS confirm this general picture. In 11:2 W and Θ read the participle (λέγων) instead of the indicative (καὶ λέγει). This is a stylistic improvement which avoids the familiar Markan fondness for paratactic construction.[18] It may have been prompted by the fact that the Matt 21:2 and Luke 19:30 parallels prefer the participle also. The scattered supporters (OL a, Sah, 1, 13, 28, 69, 209, 346) show the reading to have little genealogical significance.

Again, in 11:15 the addition of ἐξέχεεν after κολλυβιστῶν must be a borrowing from the John 2:15 account of the temple cleansing. This reading, which unites W, Θ, Fam 13, 28, 565, and 700 among the Caesareans, is supported also by N, Σ, and the Geo. The B reading appears awkward in comparison with the W-Θ variant, which supplies a verb for τὰς τραπέζας. The insertion of ἐξέχεεν from the familiar Johannine account is neither very surprising nor very significant.

In 11:31 the reading ἐρεῖ ἡμῖν unites not only the most notable "Caesareans" (W, Θ, Fam 13, Fam 1, 565, 700) but also important Western witnesses (OL a, b, c, d, f, ff², i, k², q, and the Vg). The essential difference from the Neutral text is the addition of the pronoun, and this addition is found in D, the OL, and the Peshitto and Sinaitic Syr. Further, the addition of the pronoun obviously harmonizes Mark here with the Matt 21:25 parallel, and the W-Θ agreement is again insignificant.

The variant supported by W and Θ (with Fam 13 and 565) in 11:32 is separated from the reading of D only by the difference in voice. The sense of both readings—"we fear"—is the same and is a marked change from the Neutral reading—"they were afraid"; but the first person plural is also the reading behind the OL, Vg, Boh, Arm, and Syr (Harclean). Further, the reading harmonizes the Markan passage with the Matt 21:26 parallel. The major Greek variants are set forth

---

[18]Is this fondness an example of "Semitic flavour"? See Cranfield, *The Gospel According to Saint Mark* 20-21; V. Taylor, *The Gospel According to St. Mark* 48-49, 57-58.

here to show how much the Caesarean reading accords with the Western witnesses, and is therefore either a "Western" reading or an insignificant harmonization.

א, B, A, TR	ἐφοβοῦντο
W, Θ, 565, Fam 13	φοβούμεθα
D	φοβοῦμεν (OL also)

The W-Θ agreements in Mark 11, then, yield the same unimpressive picture. W and Θ agree in many Western readings and/or variants easily accounted for as common scribal handling of Mark.

Mark 12

In Mark 12 W and D are noticeably less close in their relationship to each other (Mark 11: 36.5%; Mark 12: 25.2%), yet W and Θ retain about the same agreement. Here are the quantitative relationships of W and Θ for this chapter.

W-13	= 54.4%		Θ-565	= 76.7%
W-Θ	= 44.7%		Θ-13	= 46.6%
W-TR	= 40.8%		Θ-W	= 44.7%
W-565	= 40.8%		Θ-D	= 41.7%
W-א	= 37.9%		Θ-א	= 38.8%
W-A	= 35.9%		Θ-TR	= 37.9%
W-B	= 35.9%		Θ-B	= 36.9%
W-D	= 25.2%		Θ-A	= 35.0%

It is clear that the quantitative relationship of W with Θ is in no way significantly strong. Of the forty-three agreements of W with Θ, D supports fourteen. The Neutral MSS support sixteen (B) or twenty (א) agreements of W with Θ. The figures suggest that the agreement of W with Θ in Mark 12 is not so clearly accounted for by their joint support of Western readings. This may be confirmed in a study of the agreements of W with Θ against the "non-Caesarean" control witnesses.

In 12:1 W and Θ (with Fam 13 and 565) agree in reading ἄνθρωπός τις ἐφύτευσεν ἀμπελῶνα. This is a different word order compared with the other readings and is further distinguished by the presence of the indefinite pronoun. It is interesting to observe that both these characteristics seem to be derived from the Matthean parallel (Matt 21:33). It is especially interesting to see that in Matt 21:33 the indefinite pronoun τις rather than ὅστις is supported by scattered Western witnesses (OL e, f, h, Syr). The presence of τις in Mark 12:1 in W and Θ may be a harmonization to a "Western" Matthean text.

Another harmonization which distinguishes W, Θ, and 565 from the other witnesses in 12:1 is the addition of αὐτῷ after περιέθηκεν. The Matt 21:33 parallel has the pronoun αὐτῷ, and familiarity with the Matthean reading must account for its presence in W, 565, and Θ at Mark 12:1. The Isaiah 5 (LXX) passage to which allusion is made in Mark 12 does not account for either of the W-Θ variants.

In 12:6 the reading uniting W, Θ, and 565 against the others at the beginning of the verse, ὕστερον δέ, is obviously borrowed from the Matt 21:37 parallel. Conflations of this harmonization with the Markan ἔτι produce the reading of Fam 13 here—ὕστερον δὲ ἔτι. The fact that the same basic harmonization appears but with the slight difference indicated here may be taken as a hint that the agreement among all these witnesses probably originated in coincidental harmonization.

The variant distinguishing W, Θ, Fam 13, and 565 from the rest in 12:15 is an addition of ὑποκριταί after πειράζετε harmonizing the statement with the Matt 22:18 parallel. The same harmonization is supported by P[45], Fam 1, 28, F, G, N, Σ, OL q, Vg, Syr (Harclean), Sah, Geo, and Arm. The occurrence of this variant in such a wide range of MSS suggests only the popularity of the harmonization. This means the variant is worth little in showing genetic relationships.

Again, in 12:30 the words W and Θ share at the end of the verse, αὕτη πρώτη, come from Matt 22:38. A very similar harmonization, αὕτη πρώτη ἐντολή, is supported by Fam 1, Fam 13, 700, D, the Byzantine text, the OL, Vg, Syr, and Arm. The reading of W and Θ is only superficially distinctive, and fails to show a special W-Θ relationship.

The harmonizations cited here cannot be called evidence for a Caesarean textual agreement between W and Θ, for the agreements of these two witnesses must be seen in the wider context of the harmonistic treatment of Mark by many scribes.

In 12:19 there is a minor agreement of W and Θ against the other witnesses.

W, Θ	τέκνον μὴ ἀφῇ
TR, A, Fam 13, D	τέκνα μὴ ἀφῇ
B	μὴ ἀφῇ τέκνον
ℵ	μὴ ἀφῇ τέκνα

It is easy to see that the real difference between W-Θ and the Byzantine-D alliance is the plural against a singular form. It is no greater than the same minor distance between ℵ and B. Further, the plural noun form may come from the Matt 22:24 parallel. In any case, the W-Θ reading is not really a distinctive or important agreement.

In 12:34 W, 565, and Θ agree in having ὅτι introduce Jesus' statement. The use of this word to introduce direct quotations is a Markan characteristic and could be a case where W, Θ, and 565 preserve an original reading.[19] For purposes of detecting kinship among MSS, this kind of minor stylistic variant is worthless. Unless there is a pattern of the same variant in many places, and unless the variant is uncommon in other MSS, minor agreements such as this mean little.

Another special agreement of W, Θ, and Fam 13 against the "non-Caesareans" in 12:34 must be set aside as of no consequence. Their preference for the present infinitive rather than aorist infinitive, namely ἐπερωτᾶν for ἐπερωτῆσαι, is only a mark of common stylistic variation difficult to attribute to common ancestry.

Here we may note also the agreement of W and Θ in 12:28, reading ἀκούων against ἀκούσας. This variant, a simple preference of present participle for aorist participle, is another example of the very minor readings that are found to characterize the so-called Caesareans.

The final special agreement of W and Θ (with 565 and Fam 13) in Mark 12

[19]C. H. Turner, "Marcan Usage," *JTS* 28(1927) 9-15.

is in v. 41. There these witnesses, plus Fam 1, 28, 91, 299, the Sinaitic, Harclean, and Jerusalem Syr, Arm, Geo, and Origen, read ἑστώς against καθίσας. This is a significant variant in that it does change the "sense" of the statement and has Jesus "standing," while the other witnesses have him "seated." The former term is not a harmonization with any of the other Gospels, and it is hard to say what could have prompted the origin of this variant except for the possibility of some editorial concern over Jesus sitting down in the temple area.[20] This is a striking reading, and it is not likely that the same reading is found in these several MSS by coincidence. Nearly all the major representatives of the broad range of "Caesarean" witnesses support the reading. Here at last, it might be argued, one has a hint of the genealogical relationship of all these witnesses. But how can one such reading prove such a relationship? Instead the reading shows only that all these "eastern" witnesses may be influenced by the same earlier witness (or idea?) at this point in Mark, and at this point only. It would be going beyond the evidence to call this reading a distinctively "Caesarean" reading, showing a unique text-type.

Thus, in Mark 12, while the Western affinities of the readings shared by W and Θ are less pronounced, the significance of their agreements is not thereby enhanced. These agreements are nearly all harmonizations, minor stylistic changes, or improvements which are often shared by a broad spectrum of texts current especially in the eastern part of the Mediterranean world at approximately the same time as W circulated in Egypt.

Mark 13

For convenience, here again are the quantitative relationships of W and Θ in Mark 13.

W-13	=	54.4%	Θ-565	= 76.5%
W-TR	=	47.1%	Θ-13	= 58.8%
W-A	=	42.6%	Θ-D	= 39.7%
W-B	=	42.6%	Θ-W	= 35.3%
W-ℵ	=	41.2%	Θ-TR	= 35.3%
W-565	=	41.2%	Θ-A	= 33.8%
W-Θ	=	35.3%	Θ-ℵ	= 29.4%
W-D	=	32.4%	Θ-B	= 19.1%

The reader will note that in this chapter the quantitative agreement of W and Θ is lower than in Mark 12 (44.7%). The relationship of Θ to Fam 13 is much more striking (58.8%). The relationship of W to Fam 13 (54.4%) in this chapter also makes all the more noticeable the low level of agreement of W with Θ. The obvious reason for this situation is that the readings shared by W and Fam 13 are not supported often by Θ and the Θ-Fam 13 agreements are not often supported by W. Thus it is difficult to posit a textual kinship linking all three witnesses.

For the sake of completeness it will be helpful to look closely at the

---

[20] "Die Lesart hängt vielleicht mit der späteren Bestimmung zusammen, dass man im innern Vorhof nicht sitzen durfte," Friedrich Hauck, *Das Evangelium des Markus* (Leipzig: A. Deichert, 1931) 151.

agreements that are shared by W and Θ. Of the twenty-four points of agreement counted, D is the sole supporting uncial three times. The Neutrals alone support W and Θ once. The Byzantines support them against the other textual traditions four times. D is present among supporters of W and Θ a total of ten times, and so is Codex A. B supports a total of five agreements of W and Θ.

Though D here is not so clearly predominant in its support of the W-Θ agreements, it is at least noticeably more frequent in its support than the Neutral text. Thus it is still true that the W-Θ agreements can be said to lean toward "Western" readings and away from the Neutral text.

Of the seven cases of special agreement of W with Θ against the "non-Caesarean" control witnesses, five are clear harmonizations. In 13:2 the absence of ὁ ᾽Ιησοῦς is no doubt prompted by its absence in the parallel in Matt 24:2. It is also worthy of note that the variant has the support of several OL MSS (a, b, i) as well as 565, 700, and two Vg MSS.

In 13:4 the absence of πάντα makes the passage resemble its Synoptic parallels, in which the word does not occur. This variant is not restricted to Caesarean MSS, being supported by 565, Δ, OL k, and the Sinaitic Syr.

In 13:6 the more specific reading supported by W and Θ, which adds ὁ Χριστός after ἐγώ εἰμι, is a harmonization with the Matt 24:5 parallel. The variant is supported by numerous MSS (Fam 13, 28, 565, 700, 1071, OL MSS b, c, g², Vg, Sah, Boh, Arm), several of which are Western witnesses.

In 13:26 the singular form ἐν νεφέλῃ found in Θ, Fam 13, and W, where others have ἐν νεφέλαις, harmonizes Mark with Luke 21:27. This harmonization is supported by an OL MS (k); and another variant, ἐπὶ τῶν νεφελῶν, harmonizing the passage with Matt 24:30, is supported by D and the Sinaitic Syr. This illustrates a tendency toward harmonization, but not always resulting in the same harmonizations.[21]

In 13:34 the W-Θ reading (supported by 565 and Fam 13), ὥσπερ γάρ instead of ὡς, is another harmonization, causing Mark to agree with Matt 25:14. (Almost the same harmonization, but without γάρ, is supported by Fam 1 and other witnesses.) All five of the agreements of W and Θ cited so far carry little weight in establishing a special W-Θ relationship, for they are all minor but clear harmonizations with support from representatives of the broad "Western" text.

Apart from these harmonistic readings there are two special agreements of W and Θ that must be mentioned. In Mark 13:27 W, Θ, Fam 13, and several others (U, Y, Φ, Fam 1, 28, 72, 106, 470, 473, 482, 506, 517, 565, 700) read τῆς γῆς, while the other control MSS do not have the article. The variant is obviously very insignificant and is shared by such a wide variety of witnesses that it cannot be regarded as evidence for a Caesarean text.

Finally, in 13:10 the variant attested by W, Θ, 565, OL MSS b, c, d, ff, g², i, r¹, Syr Peshitto, Sah, and Boh tends to make a noticeable change in the sense of the passage. The "W-Θ" reading is here set forth with the "B" reading for close comparison.

---

[21] "It should be observed that the harmonistic changes in the Western text as in all other texts were irregular and unsystematic"; Westcott and Hort, *The New Testament in the Original Greek: Introduction* 125.

B   καὶ εἰς πάντα τὰ ἔθνη πρῶτον δεῖ κηρυχθῆναι τὸ εὐαγγέλιον

W, Θ   καὶ εἰς πάντα τὰ ἔθνη πρῶτον δὲ δεῖ κηρυχθῆναι τὸ εὐαγγέλιον

The presence of δέ tends to break the connection between τὰ ἔθνη and the following phrase. The B reading appears to prophesy a "gentile mission." The W-Θ reading appears to remove this sense from the passage. In the latter reading, "to all the nations" should possibly be connected with the preceding phrase, which describes those to whom a testimony will have to be given in persecution. The phrase "the gospel must be preached" would then be simply a general exhortation to be busy about the work of evangelizing. Though there are other views on this textual variation, I am inclined to regard the reading of W and Θ and their supporters listed above as an editorial change made at a time when the church was predominantly gentile and when references to a "gentile mission" were strange; but whatever the reason for its origin, the reading is probably best classified as a "Western" reading here shared by W and Θ.[22] The variant is not evidence of a special W-Θ relationship.

Mark 14

In ch. 14 the W-Θ relationship is an insignificant 34.2 percent. The insignificance of their relationship is apparent also when one examines the actual agreements of these two MSS. In addition to the fact that forty of their fifty-one agreements are supported by one or more of the non-Caesarean witnesses, and are often simply "Western" readings, even where W and Θ agree against the non-Caesarean witnesses their shared readings are not impressive. Some of the places where A and TR support these "Caesareans" against the other control MSS can easily be identified as points of Western affinity. For example, in 14:9 D deserts the other Western witnesses while A, TR, W, Θ, 565, Fam 13, and numerous Westerns again agree in reading ἀμήν without δέ (OL MSS c, f, ff², g¹, i, k, l, q, plus Vg and Peshitto). In 14:27 the reading supported by A, TR, W, Θ, 565, and Fam 13 (the omission of ἐν ἐμοί ἐν τῇ νυκτί ταύτῃ) is also supported by c, g², the Vg, the Harclean and Peshitto Syr, and other versions. This too can be regarded as a "Western" reading. Careful observation, then, shows that the Western textual element is influential in ch. 14 in binding together W and Θ.

Several of the eleven agreements of W and Θ against the non-Caesareans become less impressive when one notes the reading of D and the OL at those points. In 14:61 the W-Θ reading, καὶ πάλιν, is on close examination probably a conflation of the Neutral reading πάλιν and the D reading καί.[23] In 14:65 the W-Θ reading αὐτὸν ἐλάμβανον instead of αὐτὸν ἔβαλλον, the Byzantine reading, uses the same verb found in ℵ, B, and D; but W and Θ have the verb in the imperfect, while ℵ and B have the aorist form. D also has the imperfect form of the verb but

---

[22]The passage is discussed in its variant forms by F. C. Burkitt, *Christian Beginnings* (London: University of London Press, 1924) 145-47; G. D. Kilpatrick, "The Gentile Mission in Mark and Mark 13:9-11," *Studies in the Gospels* (ed. D. E. Nineham; Oxford: Basil Blackwell, 1967) 145-58; G. R. Beasley-Murray, *A Commentary on Mark Thirteen* (London: Macmillan, 1957) 42-44; Olof Linton, "Evidence of a Second-Century Revised Edition of St. Mark's Gospel," *NTS* 14(1967/68) 321-55.

[23]See Turner's study of asyndeton in Mark, "Marcan Usage," *JTS* 28(1927) 15-19.

in a different word order with the object following the verb—ἐλάμβανον αὐτόν. This fact brings W and Θ near enough to D to justify calling the W-Θ reading "Western."

Of the remaining W-Θ special agreements, seven can be identified as simple harmonizations. The reading in 14:22 shared by W and Θ, εἶπεν αὐτοῖς rather than καὶ εἶπεν, seems to be an assimilation to the phrase in 14:24 as it is found in most Greek MSS. In v. 24, where Jesus gives the cup, most MSS read καὶ εἶπεν αὐτοῖς.[24] W and Θ surely conformed the "formula" introducing the bread to this fuller phrasing. The same assimilation is attested in 565, Δ, k, i, Syr Peshitto, and Boh. This easily shows the reading is not distinctively "Caesarean."

In 14:29 the W-Θ reading ἀποκριθεὶς λέγει instead of ἔφη has the dramatic present so familiar to Markan students (as does D) but also adds the participle, similar to the Matt 26:33 parallel.

In 14:49 the addition τῶν προφητῶν after γραφαί is a clear harmonization with the phrase in Matt 26:56, which introduces one of Matthew's familiar "formula" quotations. Support for this harmonization is chiefly from MSS connected with the Caesarean group but is not restricted to these MSS (Fam 13, 565, N, Φ, Harclean Syr, Geo, and Arm).

The use of τότε rather than καί in 14:50 seems to be prompted by a desire to avoid the repetition of the latter word several times in this passage. The τότε is also used in the Matt 26:56 parallel and is supported in Mark here by the OL and Vg as well as by Fam 13, N, 565, 1542.

In 14:54 the use of the imperfect rather than the aorist (also supported by Fam 13 and 565) is not only the reading of both parallels (Matt 26:58; Luke 22:54), but is also supported by numerous Western witnesses (OL MSS, Syr Peshitto). W-Θ and these supporters read ἠκολούθει in place of ἠκολούθησεν.

The W-Θ-Fam 13 agreement against the other witnesses in 14:64 is a fuller phrase—τὴν βλασφημίαν τοῦ στόματος αὐτοῦ for τῆς βλασφημίας. The only significant thing about the reading is the addition of the last three words, which surely must be borrowed from the Luke 22:71 parallel. Other witnesses, including other "Caesarean" witnesses, have a harmonization to the Matt 26:65 parallel as it appears in many MSS. MSS 565 and 124 (both "Caesarean") support still another harmonization. In order that these readings may be compared they are set out here.

W, Θ, Fam 13	τὴν βλασφημίαν τοῦ στόματος αὐτοῦ
D, Fam 1, q, r², Vg, Syr Sinaitic, Geo	τὴν βλασφημίαν αὐτοῦ
124, 565	τὴν βλασφημίαν αὐτοῦ ἐκ τοῦ στόματος αὐτοῦ

It will be seen that the "Caesareans" all harmonize Mark with a parallel, but they do so in three different ways! The variation in the readings makes it likely that it was a common tendency toward harmonization that caused the similarity of readings—not descent from a common archetype. This case illustrates the fact that,

---

[24]Here only B omits αὐτοῖς. This may be an assimilation in B to the 14:22 phrase which B reads, with most others, without the pronoun. Perhaps B is assimilating 14:24 to v. 22 while W and Θ assimilate in the opposite direction.

though such harmonizing often produced coincidentally identical readings, this was not always the case.

In 14:65 there is another addition to the Markan text based on parallels in Matt 26:68 and Luke 22:64. Various forms of this harmonization are found in W, Θ, Fam 13, 1071, 565, 700, N, U, X, Σ, Harclean Syr, Boh, Geo, and Arm. Though the variant is not really a W-Θ agreement, because they each support a slightly different reading (adding after προφήτευσον: νῦν [ἡμῖν Θ, 565] χριστέ τίς ἐστιν ὁ παίσας σε), this is further evidence of the harmonistic tendencies of many scribes who copied Mark.

Two agreements of W and Θ against the other control witnesses are such minor variations that they are of no genealogical significance. In 14:35 W, Θ, 565, and Fam 13 read the accusative where the other MSS have the genitive in the prepositional phrase: ἐπὶ τὴν γῆν for ἐπὶ τῆς γῆς. The preposition is commonly used with either case in the Hellenistic period, and the variation is probably due to scribal preferences.[25] In 14:51 W, Θ, 565, and Fam 13 go against the rest in reading οἱ δέ for καί. As mentioned earlier, there was a widespread tendency for scribes to substitute δέ for καί, especially where a change of subject is indicated in the narrative.[26] Neither variant qualifies as evidence of a special W-Θ relationship.

The final reading to be considered from Mark 14 is the agreement of W, 565, and Θ in 14:16 in adding ἑτοιμάσαι after ἐξῆλθον. The addition is not a harmonization but seems instead to be an editorial clarification of the departure of the disciples. The same verb (ἐξῆλθεν) is used, for example, in the Johannine account of Judas' treachery (John 13:30). Possibly because the verb had thus been "contaminated" in that it was used to describe the desertion of Judas, it was found necessary to make clear that here in Mark 14:16 the disciples "departed *to prepare*." This addition is attested also by 124, Sah, Geo, and Arm. This scattered support makes it difficult to identify the addition as a distinctive "Caesarean" reading.

The agreements of W and Θ in Mark 14 are then also largely of Western affiliation and are nearly all harmonistic or stylistic improvements of the Markan text.

Mark 15:1-12, 39-41; 16:1-8

Because Mark 15:13-38 is missing from W, and because ℵ and B end at 16:8, we will examine here, as a block, the remaining portions of chs. 15–16.

In this section W and Θ agree in twenty-eight instances. In eleven of these cases D is the only uncial support from among the control witnesses. ℵ and B each support only one W-Θ agreement against the other non-Caesarean witnesses. The Byzantines support three agreements of W and Θ against B and D. It is patently clear from this data alone that the textual element binding W and Θ together here is of predominantly Western affinity.

There are five places where W and Θ agree against the non-Caesarean control witnesses. The variant in 15:2, an addition of λέγων after Πιλᾶτος, can be attributed to any or all of the following factors: (1) it assimilates this passage

[25]BDF §§ 233-35.
[26]See other examples given by O. Linton, "Evidences," 321-55.

to the widely supported reading in Mark 15:4; (2) it harmonizes the Mark 15:2 passage with the parallels Matt 27:11 and Luke 23:3, in which the same participle occurs; (3) the participle makes the passage more "literary."[27] In any event, the variant is attested by important OL witnesses (c, k, aur) and others (Fam 13, 565, 700, Sah) and can hardly be called a "Caesarean" reading.

In 15:3 the added sentence supported by W, 565, and Θ is another harmonization to parallels in Matt 27:12 and Luke 23:9. These witnesses, plus N, U, Δ, Σ, Ψ, 1071, two Vg MSS, OL MSS a, c, Sinaitic and Harclean Syr, Geo, and Arm, add αὐτὸς δὲ οὐδὲν ἀπεκρίνατο after πολλά. In view of the widely scattered support listed above, it would seem that this reading cannot really be called a distinctive "Caesarean" reading. It is simply a popular harmonization.

In 15:39 W and Θ (and 565) agree in omitting οὕτως. This omission may have been prompted by the Matt 27:54 and Luke 23:47 parallels in which the word does not appear, and the omission is attested by the Sinaitic Syr, Geo, and Arm—all witnesses from the eastern part of the empire. This, however, hardly demonstrates genetic connections.

In 16:2 W and Θ (plus 565) support the addition of ἔτι before the genitive absolute ἀνατείλαντος τοῦ ἡλίου. This addition makes more precise an otherwise ambiguous expression of time and thus reflects an editorial correction of the Markan phrase. Such a correction may have been made independently in more than one MS, and it would be pressing the data to make this addition an evidence of a "Caesarean text." In the same vein, the preference of μνῆμα by W, Θ, 565, and Fam 13 in place of μνημεῖον in 16:2 is inconsequential.

In this final section of Mark it is again clear that where W and Θ agree, they do so often in readings shared by D and other Western witnesses. The number of W-Θ agreements that cannot be identified as readings of major textual groups is small, and what readings there are like this are of little consequence, being nearly always harmonizations or insignificant stylistic changes. So, neither in number nor in quality do the W-Θ agreements support the idea that W should be linked with Θ in a special textual relationship.

SUMMARY

In Mark 5:31–16:8, W is usually described as a Caesarean witness, but the average quantitative relationship of W and Θ in Mark 6–16 is 39.7 percent. By any stretch of the term this is not a close relationship. If by the term "text-type relationship" one means the kind of relationship shared by ℵ and B or that of A and TR, then W and Θ do not share such a relationship in Mark. The fact that Θ and 565 show an average agreement of 68.2 percent over all of Mark, a far closer agreement than either shows with any other witness used in this study, seems to indicate that these two are close allies, perhaps evidencing a "Caesarean text," but W cannot be linked with this textual tradition. The relationship of W with 565, the other major

[27]See Turner, "Marcan Usage," *JTS* 29(1928) 359-61.

Caesarean witness, is almost as weak as the W-Θ relationship, only 40.7 percent averaged over Mark 6–16, and this confirms that W is not to be regarded as even a weak member of the Caesarean group.

The average agreement of Θ and D over Mark 1–16 is 45.5 percent. While this is not a high agreement, it is a demonstrably closer agreement than that of W with Θ. Thus if W were to be classified as a Caesarean witness, D would have to be regarded as a better one, for it agrees with Θ better. Now no one would describe D as a Caesarean witness in Mark, but the data show that the supposed agreement of W with the Caesarean text has in the past been overrated. The data also raise the question of whether in fact Θ should not be classed as a secondary witness to the Western textual tradition, for the Θ-D agreement in Mark (45.5%) is only slightly less than the W-D agreement in Mark 1–4, where W is supposed to be "Western" (48.9%). It has been shown here that the bulk of the agreements of W with Θ are either supported by D or often by several OL witnesses without D. In other words, it appears that a conspicuous amount of the textual element shared by W and Θ is simply the Western textual tradition. That the textual tradition reflected in Θ is noticeably "Western" is confirmed by the agreement of 565 and D—48.6 percent over Mark 1–16—nearly identical to the W-D agreement (48.9%) in Mark 1–4. Both Θ and 565 show poor agreement with D in the first three chapters of Mark, and if we measure average agreement of Θ and 565 with D over Mark 4–16, the Western leanings of the two Caesareans become a bit more pronounced—Θ-D: 47.1 percent; 565-D: 52.3 percent.

In their article on the Caesarean text of Mark, Lake, Blake, and New described the element shared by the Caesareans as a common selection of readings, "giving now a reading from purely Neutral manuscripts, then one found only in D and the European Latin, to be followed by one peculiar to the Old Syriac or found only in the Caesarean family."[28] One gets the impression from this statement that the Caesarean text is a nearly even mixture of Western, Neutral, and Byzantine elements, with some readings all their own. The present study shows that in fact the element common to Θ and W is predominantly Western in its affinity. The foregoing scrutiny of the cases where W and Θ agree (often with Fam 13 and/or 565) against the other control witnesses (including D) shows that even in these cases these agreements are almost invariably (1) readings supported by several "Western" witnesses (OL and Old Syr), and/or (2) harmonizations of the Markan passage with the more familiar Matthean and Lukan parables, and/or (3) minor improvements in Markan style when compared with the Neutral text readings.

W and Θ (and 565) should properly be regarded as simply witnesses to the "Western" textual influence in "Eastern" MSS. There seems to be no reason to regard W as an early form of the so-called Caesarean text. The only links between W and Θ are tendencies common to many MSS (e.g., harmonization), plus the above-mentioned body of recognizable Western readings. Although it is not emphasized in this study, it should not be overlooked that a large number of the agreements of W and Θ are also supported by the Syr. Many scholars place the Syr among the witnesses to a variety of the Western text, and if this is a correct description of the Syr versions, their frequent support of W-Θ agreements might

---

[28] "The Caesarean Text of Mark," 257.

substantiate the argument presented here that these agreements are to a large degree Western readings. That is, W and Θ might be regarded as varying representatives of a text in Greek similar to that textual treatment found in the Syr.[29]

If it is true that W and Θ agree most frequently in Western variants, why do the two MSS agree so poorly in the early part of Mark where W has so many Western readings (W-Θ in Mark 1–5 = 34.6%)? There W is much closer to D, and one might expect therefore a closer agreement with Θ. In Mark 1 W and Θ are in agreement 43.2 percent; yet in Mark 2–3 W and Θ agree far less. Why this variation in agreement?

A study of the tables (Appendix I) for these chapters of Mark will show that in Mark 1, where W and Θ agree 43.2 percent, the relationship of W with D is 44.3 percent and that of Θ with D is 48.7 percent. In ch. 2, where W and D agree 46.8 percent, Θ agrees with D only 36.2 percent, and W and Θ agree only 26.1 percent. In ch. 3 W and D agree 46.9 percent; D and Θ agree 32.8 percent; and W and Θ agree only 28.1 percent. The obvious change in these last two chapters, compared with Mark 1, is the much lower relationship between D and Θ, and this is what accounts for the poor relationship of W with Θ. The two poor relationships are not coincidental. Θ is a much poorer Western witness in Mark 2–3, and thus W and Θ agree much less. This only confirms the rule observed in the closer analysis in the preceding pages, i.e., that both W and Θ have to be comparatively close to D for them to have a noticeable relationship with each other.

The connection of W and Θ in a special textual relationship is untenable. W is *not* a Caesarean MS. A description of what kind of witness Codex W is involves the investigation of its relationships with its major "pre-Caesarean" allies in the following pages.

---

[29]Hedley ("The Egyptian Texts of the Gospels and Acts," 38) described the "Caesarean" witnesses as representatives of "the general treatment of the Gospel text in the East during the first two or three centuries." On the Syr, see now B. M. Metzger, *The Early Versions of the New Testament* (Oxford: Clarendon, 1977) 3-98.

CHAPTER IV

CODEX W AND FAMILY 13

THE PROBLEM

Family 13, as indicated earlier, has been classified with Codex W and P[45] in the "pre-Caesarean" subgroup. In the preceding chapter we have seen that it is not proper to link Codex W with the later Caesarean text as represented by Codex Θ. It is now our task to study the relationship of Codex W with Fam 13. First, we will seek to discover how closely W is related to Fam 13, noting whether the relationship is close enough to justify linking them in a common group. Second, it will be of interest to analyze the *kind* of readings they share. The readings that W and Θ have in common have been found to be of definite Western tendency. What is the nature of the textual element binding W and Fam 13? If the latter two witnesses do represent an Old Egyptian text, a close analysis of their shared readings will tell its quality and usefulness in the work of textual criticism.

THE DATA

Mark 1 – 5

Here are the quantitative relationships of W and Fam 13 for Mark 1–5.

Mark 1

W-TR	= 48.9%		13-565	=	69.3%
W-D	= 44.3%		13-TR	=	55.7%
W-A	= 43.2%		13-A	=	51.1%
W-Θ	= 43.2%		13-Θ	=	45.5%
W-B	= 38.6%		13-א	=	38.6%
W-565	= 34.1%		13-D	=	38.6%
W-13	= 33.0%		13-B	=	36.4%
W-א	= 30.7%		13-W	=	33.0%

Mark 2

W-D	= 46.8%		13-TR	=	68.1%
W-א	= 34.8%		13-A	=	65.2%
W-B	= 30.4%		13-565	=	62.3%
W-A	= 27.5%		13-א	=	43.5%
W-TR	= 26.1%		13-Θ	=	39.1%
W-Θ	= 26.1%		13-D	=	34.8%
W-565	= 24.6%		13-B	=	30.4%
W-13	= 23.2%		13-W	=	23.2%

Mark 3

W-D	=	46.9%		13-TR	=	54.7%
W-13	=	28.1%		13-A	=	54.7%
W-Θ	=	28.1%		13-Θ	=	51.6%
W-ℵ	=	28.1%		13-565	=	51.6%
W-B	=	28.1%		13-B	=	46.9%
W-565	=	25.0%		13-ℵ	=	39.1%
W-A	=	23.4%		13-D	=	34.4%
W-TR	=	23.4%		13-W	=	28.1%

Mark 4

W-D	=	57.9%		13-TR	=	61.6%
W-Θ	=	42.1%		13-A	=	56.8%
W-13	=	35.8%		13-565	=	55.8%
W-565	=	34.7%		13-Θ	=	47.4%
W-B	=	27.4%		13-B	=	41.1%
W-A	=	26.3%		13-ℵ	=	38.9%
W-ℵ	=	25.3%		13-W	=	35.8%
W-TR	=	23.2%		13-D	=	30.5%

Mark 5

W-13	=	48.8%		13-TR	=	51.2%
W-A	=	47.6%		13-ℵ	=	53.6%
W-B	=	45.2%		13-B	=	52.4%
W-ℵ	=	42.9%		13-A	=	50.0%
W-TR	=	42.9%		13-Θ	=	48.8%
W-565	=	36.9%		13-W	=	48.8%
W-Θ	=	33.3%		13-565	=	36.9%
W-D	=	27.4%		13-D	=	28.6%

We will now follow the same procedure as employed in the preceding chapter to study the W-Fam 13 relationship. Over the whole of Mark 1–4 the tables will show that the quantitative relationship of Codex W and Fam 13 is not outstanding. It is in Mark 5 that Fam 13 emerges as the closest ally of W. In nearly all of Mark, Fam 13 is not related to D in any appreciable degree, and the fact that W and Fam 13 begin to draw together in Mark 5 is further evidence that there is a significant textual change in W in the latter part of this chapter and that the change is a lessening of the agreement of W with D and the Western text.

The average relationship of W and Fam 13 in Mark 6:1–16:8 is 58.1 percent. This is a much closer relationship than that of W and Θ over the same part of Mark (39.7%), and for W only the agreement with P[45] (68.9%), in the passages in which the latter was used, exceeds the quantitative relationship with Fam 13.[1]

In ch. 5 of Mark, as noted above, W begins to draw closer to Fam 13. Although their relationship there is still not exceptionally close (48.8%), it will be helpful to note the nature of this growing relationship. Of the forty-one agreements

[1]See the chart in Appendix I.

of W with Fam 13 counted in Mark 5, D supports ten; 565 supports fifteen; Θ supports sixteen; ℵ supports twenty-one; B supports twenty-two; A supports twenty-three; and TR supports twenty-two agreements. This shows that no one textual tradition gives prominent support to the W-Fam 13 agreements, and specifically that Western influence upon the readings shared by W and Fam 13 is not nearly so prominent as it is in the agreements of W with Θ. Let us now examine the seven cases where W and Fam 13 agree against all the control witnesses in Mark 5.

In Mark 5:11 W and Fam 13 have a word order all their own. The principal variants are set forth below.

TR, ℵ	πρὸς τὰ ὄρη ἀγέλη χοίρων μεγάλη βοσκομένη
W, Fam 13	ἀγέλη χοίρων μεγάλη πρὸς τῷ ὄρει βοσκομένη
A	ἀγέλη χοίρων μεγάλη βοσκομένη πρὸς τῷ ὄρει
B, 565, Θ	πρὸς τῷ ὄρει ἀγέλη χοίρων μεγάλη βοσκομένη
D	πρὸς τῷ ὄρει ἀγέλη χοίρων βοσκομένη

By placing the prepositional phrase πρὸς τῷ ὄρει where they do in the sentence, W and Fam 13 seem to approach most closely to the reading of A, though a somewhat distinctive element remains. But word order is so much a matter of stylistic preference in Greek that it is unreliable in itself for determining genetic relationship.

The next two readings shared by W and Fam 13 against the other witnesses are in Mark 5:12, where the other witnesses basically agree in putting παρακαλέω in the indicative mood and λέγω in participial form. For example, the text of B reads παρεκάλεσαν . . . λέγοντες. W and Fam 13 (supported by MS 28) have a different construction: παρακαλέσαντες . . . εἶπον. This also is a simple stylistic difference, and it has already been noted in the preceding chapter how frequently the "formula" which introduces quotations is varied in MSS. That W and Fam 13 have the same "formula" is interesting, but this must be supported by other evidence.

In Mark 5:22 W and Fam 13 read the compound verb προσπίπτει in place of πίπτει. It is interesting to note that D reads προσέπεσεν—the same compound verb but in the aorist tense. A glance farther down the Markan narrative shows that in the pericope of the woman with an issue of blood Mark unquestionably wrote προσέπεσεν to describe her approach to Jesus (5:33). The D reading in 5:22 is possibly an assimilation of this verse to the usage in 5:33; or, the use of the compound verb could reflect a simple scribal preference. The reading of W and Fam 13 may also be influenced by the same motives, but they retain the more characteristically "Markan" historic present use of the verb.[2] In any case, the very similar D variant makes the W-Fam 13 variant less valuable as evidence of a special textual relationship.

In 5:33 W and Fam 13 add ἔμπροσθεν πάντων after εἶπεν αὐτῷ, and thus make it plain that the woman spoke publicly about her actions. The parallel

---

[2]It is possible that this use of the historic present shows some slight Attic tastes in the scribes of W and Fam 13; see G. D. Kilpatrick, "Style and Text in the Greek New Testament," *Studies in the History and Text of the New Testament in Honor of Kenneth W. Clark* (ed. B. L. Daniels and M. J. Suggs; SD 29, 1967) 154.

in Luke 8:47 states that she announced herself ἐνώπιον παντὸς τοῦ λαοῦ. This may provide the source for the reading in W and Fam 13. Note, however, that the reading in W and Fam 13 is not a simple harmonization to the parallel but appears to be a more individualistic "improvement" of Mark on the general basis of the Lukan narrative. The fact that this is not a simple harmonization gives some importance to this agreement as evidence of special W-Fam 13 connections.

Also, in 5:33 W and Fam 13 read that the woman told Jesus αἰτίαν αὐτῆς. Other MSS read here τὴν ἀλήθειαν. The latter reading may have seemed vague to scribes, and the Lukan parallel (8:47) supplied a fitting substitute. Similar harmonizations and clarifications of the passage here in Mark appear in some of the versions (Sah, Geo, Arm, OL MSS c, q, e), but the bulk of the textual evidence supports the word ἀλήθειαν. The reading in W and Fam 13 is so scattered in its support that it cannot be attributed to any one textual tradition.

In 5:40 W and Fam 13 add εἰδόντες ὅτι ἀπέθανεν after αὐτοῦ. It is a direct harmonization based on Luke 8:53 and was favored by only a few witnesses (543, Sah).

The evidence from Mark 5 concerning the relationship of W and Fam 13 is so scanty that only the following summary can be made. The agreements of W and Fam 13 against the other control witnesses are not heavily supported by other witnesses and hence may be evidence of some distinctive relationship. The variants all appear to be "improvements" in comparison to the Neutral readings, sometimes in the form of harmonization with the Synoptic parallels, and this means that these W-Fam 13 agreements are probably not part of the authentic Markan text.

Mark 6

There are ninety-four agreements of W and Fam 13 in Mark 6, and here are the quantitative relationships of these two witnesses in this chapter.

W-13	= 61.8%		13-TR	=	67.1%
W-TR	= 53.9%		13-A	=	66.4%
W-A	= 51.3%		13-W	=	61.8%
W-B	= 42.8%		13-Θ	=	44.1%
W-Θ	= 41.4%		13-B	=	44.1%
W-565	= 37.5%		13-ℵ	=	43.4%
W-ℵ	= 36.8%		13-565	=	40.1%
W-D	= 34.2%		13-D	=	35.5%

TR and A support the W-Fam 13 agreements sixty-five times and sixty-three times respectively, more frequently by far than do the other witnesses. Compare this with the support by B (forty-three times) or D (thirty-three times). Θ supports them forty-four times, and 565 does thirty-eight times. These figures show that the readings shared by W and Fam 13 in Mark 6 are most frequently of Byzantine affinity.

From the four cases where W, Fam 13, and Θ agree against the other control witnesses it becomes even clearer that the first two witnesses are not to be linked with the Caesarean text. In 6:13 W, Fam 13, Θ, and 565 read ἐθεράπευον αὐτούς, while others omit the latter word. Without the pronoun the statement could seem incomplete, and the presence of the pronoun is, therefore, simply a stylistic correction. In 6:39 the reading συμπόσια συμπόσια is shortened by W, Fam 13, Θ, L, and 565 to συμπόσια. The longer reading may have seemed colloquial and wordy, for another similar attempt to improve the phrase at this point is found in D, which reads κατὰ τὴν συμποσίαν, and some such stylistic improvement lies behind the OL witnesses. The W-Fam 13-Θ reading is an "easier" reading than the Neutral text reading, and it is not difficult to imagine such an improvement occurring to the minds of scribes independently.[3]

In 6:48 W, Fam 13, Θ, 28, 700, and the Syr Peshitto add σφόδρα after ἐνάντιος αὐτοῖς. (565 reads σφόδρα but omits αὐτοῖς.) The word is not a harmonization to Synoptic parallels. It is, however, a term more common in Matthew than in any other Gospel.[4] The presence of the term in Mark in this instance could be called an assimilation to general Matthean vocabulary. It *is* a significant agreement in that only the above "Eastern" witnesses support the addition.

Virtually the same group of witnesses add οἱ ἄνδρες τοῦ τόπου at the end of Mark 6:54. This is a direct harmonization to Matt 14:35. Practically the identical harmonization appears in MSS A, G, Δ, Fam 1, 1071, c, Sah, Geo, and Arm. These latter MSS add ἐκείνου after τόπου and thus make the harmonization more complete. The reading is therefore of scant value in attesting any special relationship of any of these witnesses.

These agreements as a whole cannot be used to overturn the basic picture of the relationships of W and Fam 13 with Θ as they appear in the quantitative tables. W and Fam 13 do agree sufficiently in this chapter (61.8%) to allow one to see some obvious connection, but Θ is not related to either of them sufficiently closely to allow one to speak of any special relationship which might connect all three.

There remain five places where W and Fam 13 agree against *all* the control witnesses, including Θ and 565.

In Mark 6:4 W and Fam 13 (also 28, one Vg MS, and Geo) omit αὐτοῖς, which is found in the other MSS after ἔλεγεν. This may be described as an attempt at concise expression. In 6:6 W and Fam 13 (also L, 543, 76, 235, 247, Geo, and Arm) agree in a word order that is reversed from the reading in other MSS. The W-Fam 13 phrase is κύκλῳ κόμας. It is doubtful that either of these agreements of W and Fam 13 is of any real significance as proof of a distinctive genetic relationship. The widely scattered witnesses show that both readings are fairly random in occurrence.

Another rather insignificant agreement of W and Fam 13 is the preference for the imperfect form παρήγγελλεν over the aorist form read in other MSS in Mark 6:8.

In 6:35 the full phrase προσελθόντες αὐτῷ οἱ μαθηταὶ αὐτοῦ is supported by the Neutral witnesses and TR. Here are the variants found in the other MSS consulted:

[3]While the repetition to express distribution is perhaps "not un-Greek," it is much less "elegant," and it may be due to Semitic influence. See BDF §§158, 493; C. F. D. Moule, *An Idiom-Book of New Testament Greek* (2nd ed.; Cambridge: Cambridge University, 1963) 182.

[4]The term is used seven times in Matthew, once in Mark (16:4), and once in Luke, according to *A Concordance to the Greek Testament* (ed. W. F. Moulton and A. S. Geden; 4th ed. revised by H. K. Moulton; Edinburgh: T. & T. Clark, 1963) 927.

W, Fam 13	προσελθόντες αὐτῷ οἱ μαθηταί
A	προσελθόντες οἱ μαθηταὶ αὐτῷ
D, Θ, 565	προσελθόντες οἱ μαθηταὶ αὐτοῦ

The W-Fam 13 reading is closest to that of A, but has a different word order. All these variants reflect attempts at more concise expression compared with the Neutral reading. The W-Fam 13 reading is somewhat distinctive, and it is interesting that in this problem phrase they do agree.

In 6:55 W and Fam 13 read περιέδραμον εἰς ὅλην τὴν χώραν, while other MSS do not have εἰς. Any suspicions that the variant might indicate direct genealogical connection between these two witnesses must be balanced by the fact that the variant is only a slight "clarification" of the Markan phrase by adding a preposition. The source for the clarification is found in the Matt 14:35 parallel, which contains the preposition εἰς.

These agreements show few variants supported only by W and Fam 13 that cannot be explained as harmonizations or commonly attested improvements in Markan style. These rather lackluster agreements of W with Fam 13, however, are only a part of an overall good agreement of the two witnesses in Mark 6 as can be seen from the quantitative tables. These two MSS have a much closer agreement than do W and Θ, for example.

Mark 7

Of the forty-six agreements of W and Fam 13 counted in this chapter of Mark, none is supported exclusively either by D or by the Neutral witnesses. In comparison, TR and A support W and Fam 13 four times against the other control witnesses (and twice more with 565). TR supports W and Fam 13 a total of thirty-four times, and A does so thirty-two times. Θ supports them twenty-three times. D is present among supporters twenty-six times and B only fourteen times. These figures make clear that the readings shared by W and Fam 13 are more noticeably the readings supported by Byzantine witnesses. This confirms the observation made concerning the W-Fam 13 agreements in Mark 5–6. There we noted that the Byzantine witnesses seemed to be more constant in their support of W and Fam 13.

There are no special agreements of W, Fam 13, and Θ against the others in this chapter of Mark, though there are three agreements of W and Fam 13 against all the other control witnesses. Codex W and Fam 13 prefer the simple verb ἐρωτῶσιν in Mark 7:5 over the compound form ἐπερωτῶσιν. In 7:25 the Neutral reading, ἧς εἶχεν τὸ θυγάτριον αὐτῆς πνεῦμα ἀκάθαρτον, is a difficult expression, and, together with P[45], D, ℵ, 565, and Θ, W and Fam 13 do not read the redundant αὐτῆς.[5] In addition, W and Fam 13 (with P[45] and 28) alter the description of the troubled daughter. The W-Fam 13 reading is thus—ἧς εἶχεν τὸ θυγάτριον ἐν πνεύματι ἀκαθαρτῷ. This final prepositional phrase is a further attempt to clarify the Markan style in this passage. It is interesting that the attempt to clarify

---

[5]The redundant style reflects Semitic idiom in which the relative pronoun is indeclinable and so requires a possessive pronoun for complete clarity. See C. F. D. Moule, *An Idiom-Book of New Testament Greek* 176; also C. E. B. Cranfield, *The Gospel According to Saint Mark* 48; V. Taylor, *The Gospel According to St. Mark* 60, 349.

the passage uses what is apparently another *Markan* expression for describing demoniacs.[6] Thus, W and its allies in this reading correct Mark by use of "Gospel"
style and not by the use of some external standard such as "Attic" taste. It is
noteworthy that W and Fam 13 share this infrequently supported variant.

The mention of Jesus spitting during the healing of the deaf mute has
caused a fair amount of textual difficulty in 7:33. Many MSS show that πτύσας
was moved around in the sentence to try to make more sense of the word. W and
Fam 13 agree in reading πτύσας εἰς τὰ ὦτα (supported by 28, Sinaitic Syr, and
Geo). It is only a matter of word order, but the variations of all the MSS are
attempts to read into the passage some explanation of how Jesus used spittle in this
healing.[7] Again, it is conspicuous that in this difficult passage W and Fam 13
agree. No harmonization can account for this.

The special agreements of W and Fam 13 must be seen in the context of
a moderate agreement of these two witnesses in Mark 7 (59.7%). These two factors—moderately good quantitative agreement plus many small agreements in conspicuous places—suggest that W and Fam 13 may be somehow related to each
other. Firm conclusions about their relationship must, however, rest upon data from
the whole of Mark.

Mark 8–9

In Mark 8 the agreements of W and Fam 13 are supported slightly more frequently
by Byzantine representatives. Codex A supports the W-Fam 13 agreements twenty-
nine times, and TR supports thirty times. Codex Θ supports twenty-seven such
agreements, and 565 supports twenty-five times. Codex D supports twenty-four
W-Fam 13 agreements. Significantly less frequently in support are B, which supports only fifteen agreements, and ℵ, which supports seventeen agreements. From
these figures a general impression is gained that the textual element shared by W
and Fam 13 in Mark 8 is a body of non-Neutral readings in which the Byzantine
witnesses are more frequent in support than any other textual representative.

Let us now study the agreements of W and Fam 13 against all the other
control witnesses in an attempt to characterize more clearly the kind of textual
element they share.

In 8:8 W and Fam 13 agree in reading ἑπτὰ σπυρίδας πληρεῖς. The
latter word is supported by a few minuscules, the OL i, and four Vg MSS. It is an
apparent harmonization with Matt 15:37. In 8:10 W and Fam 13 agree in omitting
τό before πλοῖον, but this is a somewhat minor variant.

W and Fam 13 stand (with P[45]) alone in Mark 8:11 against the other
control witnesses in reading ἐκ τοῦ οὐρανοῦ for ἀπὸ τοῦ οὐρανοῦ. This rather
minor change in prepositions may have been prompted by the Matt 16:1 and Luke
11:16 parallels. If so it is only a harmonization.

In 8:12 W and Fam 13, supported by Δ, Sinaitic and Peshitto Syr, Sah,

---

[6]ἐν πνεύματι ἀκαθάρτῳ is used only in Mark to describe demoniacs (e.g., 1:23; 5:2). Note
the discussion by O. Linton, "Evidences," 338-39.

[7]C. E. B. Cranfield, *The Gospel According to Saint Mark* 253-54, discusses ancient ideas
of the medicinal value of spittle. The "clarification" in W-Fam 13 may be based on the use of spittle
by Jesus according to Mark 8:23. See also Taylor, *The Gospel According to St. Mark* 354.

Geo, and Ethiopic witnesses, read οὐ δοθήσεται, while many other MSS have εἰ δοθήσεται. The latter reading may reflect Semitic idiom (אם).[8] The εἰ reading may have appeared strange to some Greek-speaking people and so was altered. The same alteration was made by the writers of the Matt 16:4 and Luke 11:29 parallels, and so the reading οὐ may be a harmonization in the MSS that bear it. The wide array of witnesses supporting the W-Fam 13 variant makes it common property of several textual traditions. In 8:14 W and Fam 13 agree in reading μόνον ἔχοντες ἄρτον, a reading much like that supported by P[45], Θ, and 565, except that the last two words are reversed in these witnesses.

In 8:15 the reading καὶ τῆς ζύμης is altered to καὶ ἀπὸ τῆς ζύμης in W and Fam 13. This addition assimilates the phrase to the preceding phrase in the Markan context—βλέπετε ἀπὸ τῆς ζύμης. The presence of the second ἀπό is not necessary and is an interesting agreement of W and Fam 13.

W and Fam 13 agree (with P[45] too) in Mark 8:17 by adding ἐν αὐτοῖς ὀλιγόπιστοι after τί διαλογίζεσθε. The variant is a clear harmonization with the Matt 16:8 parallel. There is evidence of a different harmonization in D and the OL MSS which add, at the same place in the text, ἐν ταῖς καρδίαις ὑμῶν from parallels in Mark 2:8; Luke 5:22; Matt 9:4.[9]

In Mark 8:18 W and Fam 13 omit καί from the phrase οὐκ ἀκούετε καὶ οὐ μνημονεύετε. This has an effect similar to the substitution of οὐδέ for οὐ, the reading in Codex D. The reading of P[45] and Θ here, οὔπω νοεῖτε οὐδὲ μνημονεύετε, harmonizes the Markan passage with the Matt 16:9 parallel. All of these variants attempt to remove the repetition of καί. W and Fam 13 do so without adding anything to the Markan passage. Their reading is not a harmonization and is another conspicuous agreement where there are several variants.

The majority of MSS read in 8:23 πτύσας εἰς τὰ ὄμματα αὐτοῦ ἐπιθεὶς τὰς χεῖρας αὐτῷ ἐπηρώτα, but W and Fam 13 add καὶ before ἐπιθείς. This addition is supported by P[45], G, Fam 1, 28, and the OL MSS c, b, d, and is an obvious attempt to smooth out the asyndeton which results when the connective is absent. This addition reveals a common editorial treatment of Mark's style.

In 8:28 W and Fam 13 read οἱ μὲν Ἰωάννην rather than ὅτι Ἰωάννην. Later in the verse they are joined by D and Θ in reading ἄλλοι δὲ Ἡλίαν rather than καὶ ἄλλοι Ἡλίαν. These two variants attempt to emphasize that the names being mentioned are alternatives being voiced as to the identity of Jesus. The change may have also been prompted by the fact that the Matt 16:14 and Luke 9:19 parallels prefer the more literary construction. There is nothing particularly distinctive about the W-Fam 13 reading here, since it reflects common scribal changes in Mark.

In 8:29 W and Fam 13 add ὁ υἱὸς τοῦ Θεοῦ τοῦ ζῶντος after Χριστός. א adds instead a shorter form, ὁ υἱὸς τοῦ Θεοῦ. Both of these changes are clear harmonizations with the Matt 16:16 parallel. The reading of W and Fam 13 is shared by Syr and Sah witnesses, but the agreement of some or all these witnesses may be due to coincidental harmonization.

Another example of such harmonizations is found in Mark 8:31 where W,

---

[8]See Taylor, *The Gospel According to St. Mark* 362-63; Cranfield, *The Gospel According to Saint Mark* 259.

[9]Θ and 565 here add ἐν ταῖς καρδίαις ὑμῶν ὀλιγόπιστοι, which looks like a harmonization conflating readings like those of W-Fam 13 and D.

Fam 13, and Boh read καὶ ἀπὸ τότε rather than the simple καί at the beginning of the verse. The longer connective phrase is probably borrowed from Matt 16:21 and is, then, a harmonization.

There is nothing very striking about the agreements which have been discussed here. In a few cases, however, W and Fam 13 conspicuously agree where MSS show several variants. Again, one should keep in mind that in Mark 8 W and Fam 13 have a 61 percent agreement, which is probably evidence of some special relationship shared by them, although they do not exhibit a relationship anywhere in Mark as close as א and B, or TR and A.

Mark 9 shows a diminished but still noticeable agreement of W with Fam 13 (53.0%). Of their seventy agreements in this chapter of Mark, 565 supports thirty-three; Θ supports twenty-nine; TR supports twenty-nine; Codex A supports twenty-eight; B and א support them twenty-two times; and D agrees twenty times. 565 is the most frequent supporter, but this should not be taken to mean that there is a distinctive agreement of W, 565, and Fam 13 here. Most of the agreements of 565 and Θ with W and Fam 13 are also supported by the Byzantines.

There are fourteen agreements of W and Fam 13 against all the other representatives used in this study. W and Fam 13 add ὁ Ἰησοῦς after μετεμορφώθη in Mark 9:2 (supported also by P45). The addition or omission of Jesus' name appears frequently in the textual tradition of the NT, and agreement in such a common scribal change is not in itself conspicuous.[10]

The agreement of W and Fam 13 in 9:7, reading ἐπισκιάζουσα αὐτούς rather than ἐπισκιάζουσα αὐτοῖς, is supported by a scattering of witnesses (H, U, 28, other minuscules). It is probably based on the usage of the accusative form in Matt 17:5; Luke 9:34.

In 9:9 W, Fam 13, 28, and 700 read ἐξηγήσωνται rather than διηγήσωνται. It is difficult to find substantive difference between the two readings, and the variation may be a coincidental scribal preference in vocabulary.

The agreement of W and Fam 13 in 9:17 is a simple difference in word order from the bulk of MSS—ἐκ τοῦ ὄχλου εἷς, rather than εἷς ἐκ τοῦ ὄχλου.

In 9:19 W and Fam 13 (supported by P45 and other scattered witnesses) add καὶ διεστραμμένη after ἄπιστος. The parallels in Matt 17:17 and Luke 9:41 are obvious sources for this variant and it is a harmonization.

In 9:21 W, Fam 13, 28, OL MSS a and f, and three Vg MSS add λέγων after τὸν πατέρα αὐτοῦ. Θ and 565 add a longer variant—ὁ Ἰησοῦς λέγων. Both variants are common improvements of the Markan text, and the same "improvements" can be observed in the handling of the Markan material by Matthew and Luke.[11] The agreement is not significant in itself.

There is the insignificant preference of the aorist εἶπεν rather than the imperfect form of the verb in 9:24, supported by W, Fam 13, P45, OL MSS a, f, k, q, and the Sinaitic Syr.

In 9:25 the reading of the mass of MSS, ἐπισυντρέχει, is altered to a simpler συντρέχει in W and Fam 13. The former word is not found elsewhere in

---

[10]See Richard C. Nevius, *The Divine Names in the Gospels* (SD 30; Salt Lake City: University of Utah, 1967) 87-88.

[11]See the study of the relative absence of λέγων in Mark by Turner, "Marcan Usage," *JTS* 29(1928) 359-61.

the NT.[12] The latter word is, no doubt, an improvement of the statement to a more familiar vocabulary. The fact that only W and Fam 13 have this variant does make this agreement conspicuous.

In 9:33 W and Fam 13, with the support of Fam 1 and Codex 28, read the aorist passive διελέχθητε πρὸς ἑαυτούς, while all other witnesses have the imperfect διελογίζεσθε. In 9:34 a phrase similar to that used here by W and Fam 13 occurs—πρὸς ἀλλήλους γὰρ διελέχθησαν; the W-Fam 13 reading in 9:33 is therefore probably a simple assimilation to the latter phrase.

W and Fam 13 agree also in 9:34, reading τίς αὐτῶν μείζων εἴη. The more likely Markan text has simply τίς μείζων. The reading of W and Fam 13 appears to be a harmonization with the Luke 9:46 parallel. This is, however, an interesting agreement, since MSS offer several variants.

In 9:38 W and Fam 13 share two readings which are really parts of one "correction" of Mark. While most MSS of the non-Neutral text-types have ἀποκρίθη . . . λέγων introducing the quotation, W and Fam 13 read ἀποκριθεὶς . . . εἶπεν. This construction is supported by the Luke 9:49 parallel and must be a harmonization. (565 also has ἀποκριθεὶς but has λέγει in place of εἶπεν.)

There is a minor change in prepositions in 9:39 where W and Fam 13 read ἐν τῷ ὀνόματί μου in place of ἐπὶ τῷ ὀνόματί μου. The W-Fam 13 reading is supported by Fam 1, Δ, OL, Vg, Syr, Sah, and Boh. The two prepositional phrases are often interchanged in the textual witnesses, and agreement in their use indicates only scribal preferences.[13]

In 9:43 W, Fam 13, Fam 1, 28, and the Sinaitic Syr omit εἰς τὴν γέενναν. The reason for this omission may have been that the parallel in Matt 18:8 does not have the phrase.

In 9:47 W and Fam 13 omit the pronoun from the expression καλόν σέ ἐστιν. This omission cannot be attributed to a desire for harmonization, since the pronoun is present in the Matt 18:9 parallel. The omission here is simply a stylistic preference which makes the sentence say "it is better" rather than "it is better for you."[14]

Mark 10

This chapter continues to reveal Fam 13 to be the closest ally of W (61.2%). The Byzantine MSS are also close supporters of Fam 13 (TR-Fam 13 agreeing 57.3% and A-Fam 13 agreeing 62.1%). Of the sixty-three agreements of W with Fam 13 counted in this chapter, Codex A supports thirty-eight; TR supports thirty-four; 565 supports twenty-eight; and Θ supports twenty-three. D supports twenty-seven agreements, while B supports twenty times, and ℵ only seventeen times. The control witnesses show by their support of the W-Fam 13 agreements that again in Mark 10 the W-Fam 13 agreements are preponderantly Byzantine readings.

[12]BGD 301; James Hope Moulton and George Milligan, *The Vocabulary of the Greek New Testament* (London: Hodder & Stoughton, 1930) 247. Cf. G. W. H. Lampe (*A Patristic Greek Lexicon* [Oxford: Clarendon, 1961] 536), who shows the word used once in *Acta Thaddaei*.

[13]Fam 13 reads ἐπί in 9:37 and ἐν in 9:38, 39. D has ἐν in 9:37, 38 and ἐπί in 9:39. W has ἐν in all three cases.

[14]Here the positive form καλόν is used comparatively, possibly under the influence of Semitic idiom; so BDF § 245.

There are a few places in ch. 10 where W and Fam 13 agree against all the other control MSS. In 10:1 W and Fam 13 read συνπορεύεται rather than the third person plural form of the verb. They also change the subject from the plural to the singular—ὄχλος. Now D and Θ also have the singular subject and verb but a different choice of verb—συνέρχεται. It is doubtful that this broad similarity is any evidence of genealogical relationship. Turner has given reason to believe that the plural—ὄχλοι—is never an original reading in Mark, though it is common in the other Synoptic Gospels.[15] It may be, therefore, that W, Fam 13, D, and Θ agree in preserving an original singular noun at this point against numerous other witnesses. At the same time the verb συνπορεύεσθαι does not seem to be a favorite Markan term, and its presence here in W and Fam 13 (and nearly all other MSS) may be due to assimilation to Lukan vocabulary or some similar editorial motive.[16]

Again, in 10:1 W and Fam 13 agree in omitting πάλιν, which appears in most MSS before ὄχλοι. This omission is supported by the OL MSS b, ff, i, and r[1]. The reason for this omission may be that the word appears again in the next clause and so may have appeared repetitious to scribes.[17]

W and Fam 13 also omit ὑμῖν in Mark 10:5 from the construction ἔγραψεν ὑμῖν, and they are supported by 28, D, and several OL witnesses. But W and Fam 13 do not really agree fully with the others inasmuch as the Western witnesses include Μωϋσῆς as the subject of the verb. Nevertheless, there does seem to be some similarity among all these witnesses in the omission of the pronoun. Pronouns are often omitted for no apparent reason, and this may be the case here. It is also possible, however, that the pronoun was omitted so that a reader would not get the impression that the Mosaic command concerning divorce was limited to Jews only. The variant has support from too wide a group of witnesses to make it evidence of a special W-Fam 13 relationship.

In 10:14 W and Fam 13 have ἐπιτιμήσας αὐτοῖς εἶπεν after καί. Θ and 565 are really in agreement, with only a slightly different word order—ἐπιτιμήσας εἶπεν αὐτοῖς. The obviously distinctive element in these variants is the presence of the participle, also supported by 28 and the Sinaitic and Harclean Syr. The Synoptic parallels at this point offer no source for the addition. It may be that this is a pure editorial insertion by these MSS, for the variant seems to have no place in the Neutral text or the primary Western witnesses. This variant may, therefore, be a bit of evidence linking the Syr with these other "Eastern" witnesses in some marginal relationship.

W and Fam 13 add ἄρας τὸν σταυρόν σου before ἀκολούθει μοι in 10:21, supported by G, Fam 1, Sinaitic and Peshitto Syr, Sah, and the OL MS a. TR and A have the addition, but in the latter two witnesses the addition follows ἀκολούθει μοι. It is clear then that the reading of W and Fam 13 here reflects Byzantine affinity and is probably an assimilation to such passages as Mark 8:34.

[15]See the study on the use of these terms by Turner, "Marcan Usage," *JTS* 26(1925) 225-31. Moulton and Geden list Mark 10:1 as the only usage of the plural ὄχλοι in the Gospel of Mark (*A Concordance to the Greek Testament* 743).

[16]Turner, "Marcan Usage," *JTS* 29(1928) 289. This would make D and Θ along with 565 and other Western witnesses the bearers of original terminology here against nearly all other Greek witnesses!

[17]πάλιν is more a favorite word of Mark than of the other Synoptic Gospels. It does occur frequently in John. See Turner, "Marcan Usage," *JTS* 29(1928) 283-87.

In 10:29 W and Fam 13 add καὶ ἕνεκεν after ἐμοῦ. The same reading is attested in the corrections in ℵ and B but is not in the original hand of these two MSS. D and Θ read ἢ ἕνεκεν here. It would seem that the reading of W and Fam 13 is therefore of little significance, since it is shared by a wide assortment of MSS.

There is another obvious improvement in Markan style in the W-Fam 13 text of Mark 10:49. There these two witnesses read θαρσῶν ἔγειρε rather than θάρσει, ἔγειρε. They are supported again by Fam 1 and 28. The variant in W-Fam 13 removes the asyndeton.

In summarizing the evidence from Mark 8–10 we may say that on the whole the agreements of W and Fam 13 are more heavily supported by the Byzantine MSS than they are by any other textual representative. Neutral support is the lightest. Further, the agreements of W and Fam 13 against the control MSS in these chapters show fairly consistent support by Fam 1 and 28. These readings are very often assimilations of a passage to a nearby passage in Mark or more often harmonizations with Synoptic parallels. When the reading cannot be called a harmonization it can be identified in almost every case as an editorial improvement upon the Markan text. Few of the W-Fam 13 agreements are striking, but when the overall quantitative agreement of W with Fam 13 is seen there does seem to be evidence of a genetic connection between W and Fam 13.

Mark 11–12

In chs. 11–12 W is clearly not the closest ally of Fam 13. Instead, the Byzantine MSS move in to take this position, especially in Mark 11.

Mark 11 reveals an agreement of 51.8 percent for W with Fam 13; in Mark 10 they had 61.2 percent agreement. Of the forty-four W-Fam 13 agreements counted in this chapter, TR supports twenty-seven and Codex A supports twenty-three; Θ supports twenty-one; 565 supports twenty-two; D supports sixteen agreements; and B supports eighteen. It seems fair to say, therefore, that again the W-Fam 13 agreements are primarily of Byzantine affinity.

In 11:5 W and Fam 13, supported by X, Σ, Fam 1, 28, and Sah read τίνες δέ rather than καί τινες. The change is prompted by a stylistic preference for δέ because a change of subject occurs here. As observed before, Mark seems to have used the connective καί far too often to suit the tastes of the other Synoptic writers for whom Mark was a source and far too often for the tastes of the scribes of Mark. The variant here is therefore of no genealogical significance.

In 11:13 W and Fam 13 (supported by 225, Sinaitic and Peshitto Syr, Sah, and Boh) share the reading εἰς αὐτήν after ἦλθεν. The variant is similar to the reading ἦλθεν ἐπ' αὐτήν in the Matt 21:19 parallel, and this may be another example of harmonization in these witnesses.

Neither of these readings in Mark 11 is very significant. They show only that W and Fam 13 agree in readings of a harmonistic nature or readings that improve Markan style.

W and Fam 13 agree 54.4 percent in Mark 12, and their fifty-six agreements are supported by TR thirty-three times, by A twenty-nine times, by Θ twenty-eight times, by 565 twenty-six times, by B nineteen times, and by D ten times.

Again it is clear that the W-Fam 13 agreements are readings preferred by Byzantine MSS.

In 12:6 W and Fam 13 read υἱὸν ἔχων τὸν ἀγαπητὸν αὐτοῦ. This reading is different from the reading of TR only in that TR does not have the article, and the W-Fam 13 reading is basically a "Byzantine" variant.

A second variant shared by W and Fam 13 against the others in 12:6 is the omission of ὅτι after λέγων. This omission is supported by L, N, Δ, Σ, and OL MSS a, b, c, as well as other witnesses. The word is a characteristic usage in Mark—the ὅτι recitative used to introduce direct quotations. The word is not used so frequently in the other Synoptic Gospels; in nearly all parallels they omit the expression, and scribes of the Gospel of Mark often made the same change.[18] This variant therefore simply links W and Fam 13 in a common stylistic preference.

W and Fam 13 omit αὐτῷ from εἶπον αὐτῷ in Mark 12:16, and the omission is made also in Fam 1, 28, Syr Peshitto, and the OL MSS a, c, ff, and k. This seems to be another case of the familiar omission of pronouns. The support of the above-listed witnesses shows that this omission is especially marked by Western witnesses.

In 12:28 W and Fam 13 (with Fam 1, 28, and Sah) read πρώτη ἐντολή. Similarly, D and Θ read ἐντολὴ πρώτη. Both variants omit πάντων, which is found in ℵ, B, and A.[19] The absence of the word in the above-listed MSS may be due to a desire for concise expression, since the shorter form adequately conveys the thought.

W and Fam 13 read οἵτινες for the οὗτοι found in other MSS in 12:40. The variant is probably a simple stylistic preference for the former word instead of the demonstrative pronoun.[20] By itself agreement in such a variant is not significant for showing textual relationships of MSS.

Finally, in 12:43 W and Fam 13 (with Fam 1, Sinaitic Syr, and the OL MSS b, c, ff, g², i, q, and aur) omit τῶν βαλλόντων from the phrase πλεῖον πάντων ἔβαλεν τῶν βαλλόντων. The omission may have been prompted by the Luke 21:3 parallel. Besides, the τῶν βαλλόντων could make the sentence seem unnecessarily wordy.[21]

For the whole of Mark 11–12 the nature of the textual element common to W and Fam 13 remains about the same. The agreements are more often supported by the Byzantine witnesses than by any other representatives from the control witnesses, and the special agreements of W and Fam 13 against all the control witnesses are clear harmonizations or equally clear editorial tendencies toward more acceptable style. Several of these special agreements are supported by OL witnesses, perhaps showing that another ingredient in the textual mixture of the W-Fam 13 kind of text is a body of Western readings.

[18]See the study on the use of this word in Mark by Turner, "Marcan Usage," *JTS* 28(1927) 9-15.

[19]TR and several others have πασῶν for πάντων. The former is a "correction," since ἐντολή is a feminine noun. The neuter form "is to be explained as a stereotyped use of the neuter genitive plural to intensify the superlative . . ." (Cranfield, *The Gospel According to Saint Mark* 377).

[20]In post-classical Greek ὅστις frequently takes the place of the simple relative pronoun. See BGD 587.

[21]W and Fam 13, with TR, read βέβληκεν rather than ἔβαλεν in the phrase cited above.

Mark 13

In Mark 13 the relationship of W with Fam 13 (54.4%) is bettered by that of Θ with Fam 13 (58.8%). Indeed, this chapter of Mark is peculiar in that only here do Θ and Fam 13 have such agreement. There are no significant special agreements of Θ and Fam 13 in this chapter except in 13:20; here these two witnesses (plus 565) read ὁ Θεὸς ἐκολόβωσεν where others have κύριος as the subject. Codex W does not have a subject specified; the understood subject of the verb in Codex W is the Θεός of the preceding phrase. The variant is Θ and Fam 13 is shared by 28, 64, 91, and 299. It is not a harmonization but seems to be an assimilation to the preceding phrase in which Θεός is the subject.[22]

We may digress for a moment to examine the nature of the Θ-Fam 13 agreements since the relationship of these two is so strong in this chapter.

It is worth noting that throughout Mark the tables (Appendix I) show that Fam 13 is not a good ally of the Neutral MSS. Now in Mark 13, where Θ is a good ally of Fam 13, Θ is at its weakest relationship with the Neutral MSS. Of the forty agreements of Θ and Fam 13 in Mark 13, Codex A supports eighteen, TR supports eighteen, W supports nineteen, D supports twelve agreements (and in two more cases D's reading is very similar to that shared by Θ and Fam 13), and B supports the Θ-Fam 13 agreements only nine times. These figures show that the Θ-Fam 13 textual element in this chapter of Mark is essentially a non-Neutral type of text. It should be remembered that outside of Mark 13 the Θ-Fam 13 relationship is not very strong at all, as the tables (Appendix I) will show. This means that Θ and Fam 13 do not appear to have a special relationship, for their interesting quantitative agreement in Mark 13 is an isolated phenomenon.

To return to the W-Fam 13 agreements in Mark 13, one may note that TR and A support twenty-two of the thirty-seven agreements, Θ supports seventeen, 565 supports twenty, B supports eleven, and D supports thirteen. These figures show that the predominant affinity of the W-Fam 13 readings continues to be Byzantine in nature.

There is a special agreement of W with Fam 13 against the rest of the control witnesses in 13:14, where W and Fam 13 read στῆκον after τὸ βδέλυγμα τῆς ἐρημώσεως.[23] This participle is one of at least four variant readings. The ℵ-B reading is ἑστηκότα, while D has ἑστηκός and TR, A, Θ, and 565 have ἑστός. The sense does not really change in any of these, and the variants are all therefore rather insignificant.

Mark 14:1 – 16:8

In the final chapters of Mark (14:1– 16:8) the quantitative relationship of W with Fam 13 varies somewhat. In Mark 14 they agree 65.1 percent, their closest agree-

---

[22]This assimilation may have been aided by the fact that κύριος came to be widely used as a title of Jesus. In 13:20 Jesus is clearly not the subject of the sentence, and so scribes may have thought Θεός the best reading. See Werner Foerster, κύριος, *TDNT* III, 1086-1095.

[23]Fam 13 adds τὸ ῥηθὲν ὑπὸ Δανιὴλ τοῦ προφήτου after ἐρημώσεως. This addition is also found in the Byzantine witnesses and several early versions and is a clear harmonization with the Matt 24:15 parallel.

ment in any chapter to that point, and in Mark 15:1–16:8 they agree 57.7 percent. In the former portion the W-Fam 13 relationship is the strongest one for either of them, but in Mark 15:1–16:8 Fam 13 is closest to the Byzantines—it agrees with TR 67.6 percent and with A 70.4 percent. From Mark 5 to the end of the book, Fam 13 is W's closest ally.[24] Yet only in Mark 8–9 and Mark 14 is W the closest ally of Fam 13. In the rest of Mark (except ch. 13) the Byzantine witnesses are Fam 13's closest allies. In all those chapters where the Byzantine witnesses are not the closest allies of Fam 13, they are clearly the next closest ally. This illustrates that Fam 13 is a witness with strong Byzantine affinity. Fam 13's relationship with the Neutral MSS is the weakest, and when W comes into comparatively close agreement with Fam 13, W is at that point in poorer agreement with Neutral MSS and in closer agreement with Byzantine witnesses.

In Mark 14 A supports fifty-two of the ninety-seven agreements of W with Fam 13, TR supports forty-seven, 565 supports forty-two, Θ supports thirty-six, B supports thirty-seven, and D supports only twenty-five. These figures again show how very often the W-Fam 13 agreements are those favored by Byzantine witnesses.

In 14:1 W and Fam 13 agree against the others in omitting ἐν from the phrase ἐν δόλῳ. (This omission is found also in Δ, Σ, Fam 1, and 28.) The Matt 26:4 parallel lacks the preposition and so may have occasioned the omission in the copying of Mark here.

In 14:4 W and Fam 13 add τῶν μαθητῶν after τινες to specify who the grumblers were. D, 565, and Θ also make specific mention of the disciples, but they do so by substituting οἱ μαθηταί for τινες. Both variants were clearly prompted by the Matt 26:8 parallel, which mentions the disciples as the grumblers.

There is an interesting case in Mark 14:9 where W and Fam 13, with 700, Harclean and Peshitto Syr, and the OL MSS a, c, d, f, i, and k add ὅτι after ὑμῖν. Here is an example of these MSS retaining (?) a ὅτι recitative, so familiar in Mark, while other MSS omit it.

In 14:10 W and Fam 13 add ἰδού after καί. This looks like an assimilation to the general vocabulary of the other Synoptic Gospels. The word ἰδού appears a few times in Mark but usually only when introducing direct statements of Jesus. Matthew and Luke use the word much more frequently and use it freely in narrative sections where there is no quotation—just the way it is used here. The agreement is interesting and may be indicative of the W-Fam 13 special ties exhibited in their quantitative relationship.

There is a minor change in word order in 14:13 where W and Fam 13 read τῶν μαθητῶν αὐτοῦ δύο. It is conspicuous that only W and Fam 13 appear to support this reading.

In Mark 14:31 W and Fam 13 read Πέτρος μᾶλλον περισσῶς ἔλεγεν ὅτι. The reading of Θ and 565 is very similar except for the absence of ὅτι. These in turn are all similar to the reading of Codex A (Πέτρος ἐκ περισσοῦ ἔλεγεν μᾶλλον) in specifying Peter as the speaker. There is also a minor special agreement of W and Fam 13 in 14:36, where they add μοῦ after πατήρ.

Next, in 14:51 W and Fam 13 read νεανίσκοι ἐκράτησαν αὐτόν. Θ, 565, Fam 1, and Sinaitic Syr have the same wording but with the verb in the present

---

[24]This does not include P⁴⁵. See Chapter V for the relationship of W with this witness.

tense. For that matter the Byzantines have the same reading as Θ and 565 but in a different word order. The addition of νεανίσκοι in all these witnesses against א, B, and D is perhaps an editorial clarification of the phrase, which in the latter MSS does not have a subject specified.

There is some slight evidence of Western affiliation in the variant of W and Fam 13 in 14:62, where they read ἀποκριθεὶς εἶπεν αὐτῷ, while the Neutrals and Byzantines have only εἶπεν. The reading of D and Θ is ἀποκριθεὶς λέγει αὐτῷ. It is obvious that there is similarity between the W-Fam 13 reading and that of D and Θ in the addition of the participle.

In 14:65 W and Fam 13, with Fam 1, Sinaitic Syr, and Arm, omit αὐτῷ from the phrase λέγειν αὐτῷ. In view of the several successive uses of the third person pronoun in the immediate context, scribes may have felt that the αὐτῷ in question was unnecessary and redundant. It is interesting that the Matt 26:68 and Luke 22:64 parallels do not have the pronoun here either. The omission of αὐτῷ may be a harmonization. Also in 14:15 W and Fam 13 agree in adding νύν χριστέ τίς ἐστιν ὁ παίσας σε after προφήτευσον. Θ and 565 have a very similar reading, the only difference being ἡμῖν for νύν. Both readings are harmonizations of the passage with the Matt 26:68 parallel.

The use of ἀναμνησθείς for ἀνεμνήσθη and the omission of καί before ἐπιβαλών in Mark 14:72 show W and Fam 13 again preferring a construction composed of a participle and finite verb over the paratactic style supported by other MSS.

For the remainder of Mark (15:1–16:8) there are forty-one agreements of W with Fam 13. Codex A supports W and Fam 13 twenty-six times and TR supports them twenty-four times. Θ supports sixteen agreements and 565 supports fourteen. B supports twenty times and D twelve times. These figures show that again in this part of the Gospel of Mark the readings shared by W and Fam 13 are predominantly those favored by Byzantine witnesses.

There are four special agreements of W with Fam 13 against the other control witnesses. In 15:1 W and Fam 13 add αὐτόν after παρέδωκαν. This same reading appears in Matt 27:2 in W and numerous non-Neutral MSS. The presence of the pronoun in this Markan passage may be a case of harmonization, or the source for this addition may be simply a scribal preference for the pronoun to express the object of the verb. The W-Fam 13 agreement is not very significant.

In 15:6 W and Fam 13 read εἰώθει ὁ ἡγεμών after ἑορτήν. The longer reading is a clear harmonization with the Matt 27:15 parallel and is supported by the Sah as well as a few other scattered witnesses. W and Fam 13 also have ἀπολύειν instead of ἀπέλυεν.

Finally, in 15:7 W and Fam 13 add τότε after ἦν δέ. This addition is a less obvious, but probable, harmonization with the parallel Matt 27:16 phrase εἶχον δὲ τότε.

SUMMARY

Throughout Mark 5:1–16:8 the agreements of W with Fam 13 are most heavily supported by the Byzantine representatives. What W and Fam 13 have in common, therefore, is a textual element that can be described as primarily of Byzantine affinity.

We noted in the preceding chapter of this study that the agreements of W with Θ were most frequently supported by D and other Western witnesses. We also noted that in Mark 5:1–16:8 Θ is significantly closer to D than to any other control witness, except in Mark 12–13 where there is a closer agreement with Fam 13. This means that what W and Θ have in common is not the same as what W and Fam 13 have in common. W has a relationship with each of these two witnesses for different reasons. This fractures the so-called Caesarean text-type far more deeply than has been observed before, for there seems to be no Caesarean "pattern" of readings. As already indicated, the W-Fam 13 element leans toward the Byzantine text, while the W-Θ agreements lean toward the Western witnesses. Thus all three "Caesareans" (W, Fam 13, Θ) are mixed-text witnesses.

Family 13 shows a textual mixture that is basically Byzantine with noticeable lacings of Western readings. Θ appears to be most clearly a secondary Western witness with smaller admixtures of Byzantine and Neutral readings. W has varying mixtures of these elements in still other proportions. It should already be apparent that it is not proper to lump together into one text-type these three witnesses with such varying mixtures of text.

The special agreements of W with Fam 13 against the other control witnesses are consistent with the rest of the W-Fam 13 agreements. The special agreements, while they did not have support from the control witnesses, did not appear to be distinctive in any real sense. Very often the readings were harmonizations, and often they were supported by the OL but more often by the Syr. They were almost without exception readings tending toward clarification of the text and improvement of style. The element shared by W and Fam 13 is, then, one of a "correctionist" nature, i.e., readings produced by scribes who "edited" the text as they copied it.

This means that the element common to W and Fam 13 is a secondary kind of text inferior in its value as a bearer of the original wording of Mark. It is well on its way toward the Byzantine text-type of later times. Indeed, throughout most of Mark Fam 13 is closer to the Byzantine witnesses than to any of the other representatives used in this study. Over the whole of Mark the TR-Fam 13 agreement averages 58.6 percent, and the A-Fam 13 relationship averages 57.5 percent. By comparison the Θ-Fam 13 relationship averages 45.7 percent and the 565-Fam 13 agreement averages 48.0 percent. The agreement of W and Fam 13 averaged over Mark 5:1–16:8 is 57.2 percent, measurably stronger than the relationship of Fam 13 with the two Caesareans, and much stronger than any other relationship for W, but no stronger than the relationship of Fam 13 with the Byzantines. It is perhaps most accurate, then, to portray Fam 13 as occupying a position on an evolutionary line midway between W and the Byzantine text.

CHAPTER V

CODEX W AND P⁴⁵

In the introductory chapter we noted that Codex W is usually regarded as in closest agreement with P⁴⁵ in Mark. That is, W is believed to be the more complete representative of a text very much like that of the older but fragmentary P⁴⁵.

Our object in this chapter will be to examine the agreements of W and P⁴⁵ in Mark in order to see whether this widely-known view of the two MSS is correct.

Because P⁴⁵ is so fragmentary in Mark, we will examine only the comparatively well-preserved sections of the papyrus, namely Mark 6:37-48; 7:5-8; 7:25-35; 8:11-23; 8:36–9:5; 9:19-28.[1] These sections together contain 103 variation-units. Below are listed the quantitative relationships of P⁴⁵ and W with each of the other control witnesses used. These figures are percentages of agreement out of the total of 103 variation-units. The vertical column gives the control witnesses in the order of their relationship with Codex W, closest allies first.

	W	P⁴⁵
P⁴⁵	68.9%	—
W	—	68.9%
Fam 13	59.2%	55.3%
565	42.7%	43.7%
TR	39.8%	38.8%
D	39.8%	39.8%
Θ	37.9%	36.9%
B	35.0%	39.8%
A	35.0%	37.9%
ℵ	34.0%	36.9%

These figures show that in these variation-units, W is most closely affiliated with P⁴⁵. Fam 13 is the next closest ally of W. From the standpoint of P⁴⁵, the closest ally is W, with Fam 13 again in second place.[2]

In comparing the relationships of W and P⁴⁵ one notes that the latter is

---

[1] In the study of the agreements of W with P⁴⁵ undertaken here, no textual restorations done by Kenyon in his edition were used. Only where the actual reading of the papyrus was extant was a comparison made. This was done in order to avoid the possibility that any serious errors on the part of Kenyon in restoring the lacunae might have an effect upon the reliability of this study. See the criticism of Kenyon's restoration by Hollis W. Huston, "Mark 6 and 11 in P⁴⁵ and in the Caesarean Text," *JBL* 74(1955) 264-65.

[2] Fam 13 agrees with TR 60.2 percent and with A 57.3 percent in these same 103 variation-units. This shows that Fam 13 is as much a Byzantine witness as it is a witness to the Old Egyptian text found in P⁴⁵ and W. This very strong Byzantine element distinguishes Fam 13 from W and P⁴⁵. The significance of this will be discussed in the final pages of this chapter.

slightly closer to B than is W. This observation is of course to be qualified somewhat by the fact that the fragmentary nature of the text of P⁴⁵ makes possible only a "sampling" of its readings where they are extant. As with all such limited samples, the picture of textual relationships here given may not be entirely accurate. It does seem possible, however, that this sample is a reasonably representative picture of the text of P⁴⁵.

Among the seventy-one agreements of W with P⁴⁵ in these sections of Mark, the major control witnesses support them as follows: D—thirty-one times, 565—thirty-one times, TR—twenty-eight times, B—twenty-seven times, Θ—twenty-six times, A—twenty-five times, ℵ—twenty-five times. The textual agreements of W and P⁴⁵ cannot easily be identified as belonging predominantly to a particular text-type. It is particularly important to note that in these agreements the support of 565 and Θ is not significantly more frequent than the representatives of other textual groups.

There are seven special agreements of P⁴⁵ with W against all the other control witnesses. In 8:12 W and P⁴⁵ omit λέγω ὑμῖν. There is apparently no other support for this omission. The words are absent, however, from the parallels in Matt 16:4 and Luke 11:29. The omission is no doubt a harmonization but one distinctive to these two MSS.

In 8:14 W and P⁴⁵ agree where there are several variants, which are listed below after the Neutral-Byzantine reading.

TR, A, ℵ, B, Θ, 565	λαβεῖν ἄρτους
W, P⁴⁵	οἱ μαθηταὶ αὐτοῦ λαβεῖν ἄρτους
Fam 13	οἱ μαθηταὶ αὐτοῦ ἄρτους λαβεῖν
D	οἱ μαθηταὶ λαβεῖν ἄρτους

The effect of all the variants is to make it clear that it was the disciples, not Jesus, who forgot to take bread along. The very same clarification appears also in the Matt 16:5 parallel, probably the source of the words added in all the variants above.

In 8:38, where other MSS read τῇ γενεᾷ ταύτῃ τῇ μοιχαλίδι, W and P⁴⁵ omit ταύτῃ. They are supported by the OL MSS i, k, and n. The omission was probably prompted by a feeling that the restrictive attributive construction made ταυτῆ unnecessary and the phrase wordy. The OL support may be taken to mean that this is a Western variant; or this support may only show similar tastes in translators and copyists.

There is a second special agreement of W and P⁴⁵ in 8:38. These two, with the Sinaitic Syr, the Sah, and Boh, read καί in place of μετά before τῶν ἀγγέλων. This appears to be a harmonization with Luke 9:26. Again, this reading seems to have been read only among these "Eastern" witnesses.

In 9:1 ἄν is absent from the construction ἕως ἄν ἴδωσιν in W, P⁴⁵, and also F. Grammar calls for ἄν in such constructions, but there are examples without the particle.[3] Its absence here is therefore conspicuous and is perhaps some small indication of a textual bond uniting W and P⁴⁵.

In 9:5 the Neutral witnesses and the Byzantine witnesses have ὁ Πέτρος

[3]In the Gospels see Matt 10:23; 14:32; Luke 15:4; 22:34. Nonbiblical examples are cited in BGD 334.

λέγει after ἀποκριθείς. W and P⁴⁵ read εἶπεν Πέτρος in the same place. D, 565, Θ, and others (700, OL MSS a, b, n, Sinaitic and Peshitto Syr, and Boh) read here ὁ Πέτρος εἶπεν. This last reading is basically the reading of W and P⁴⁵ in that both readings prefer the aorist verb. The word order is a more secondary variation. The reading of W and P⁴⁵ has, therefore, some Western affinity.

Finally, in 9:25 W and P⁴⁵ with Fam 1, Sinaitic Syr, and Geo omit τῷ ἀκαθάρτῳ after τῷ πνεύματι. The most probable explanation is that the omitted words may have seemed unnecessary and for the sake of concise expression were omitted.[4] It is worth noting that in a similar phrase in Mark 9:20 all the control witnesses agree that the reading is τὸ πνεῦμα without any adjective. The variant of W and P⁴⁵ in 9:25 may be an assimilation of the latter verse to the construction in 9:20.

SUMMARY

Of all the MSS studied, P⁴⁵ is the closest ally of W in the sample where P⁴⁵ is extant. This is a confirmation of the common opinion about the mutual relationship of these two MSS.

It is suggested here that the W-P⁴⁵ text may be a kind of Neutral text in an advanced stage of "mixture," i.e., a text that has been heavily affected by tendencies most clearly evident in non-Neutral texts. This seems possible because P⁴⁵, the older witness, seems a bit closer to B than does W. This fact can be understood to show that the textual development from the earlier to the later stages in the W-P⁴⁵ text was from greater to lesser agreement with the Neutral text. In the following chapter, the discussion will focus on the singular readings of Codex W and the scribal purposes evident in these readings. These scribal purposes will indicate why and how a textual tradition that may have been originally Neutral in nature could have become so "mixed" as the text of Codex W.

Having studied the agreements of P⁴⁵ with Codex W, we have considered the three important members of the so-called pre-Caesarean group (W, P⁴⁵, Fam 13). The evidence points to the conclusion that this term "pre-Caesarean" is inappropriate. None of the three "pre-Caesarean" witnesses considered agrees with Θ or 565 especially well, and Fam 13, the latest of the three, agrees as closely with the Byzantine witnesses as it does with Codex W or P⁴⁵. These facts suggest that the text embodied in Codex W, P⁴⁵, and later in Fam 13 did not become progressively more like the text of Θ and 565; rather, the W-P⁴⁵ kind of text became progressively more like the text embodied in the TR. Just where the origins of the Θ text, the so-called Caesarean text, lie is difficult to say, but Codex W and its true allies cannot be blamed with paternity.

The exact nature of the mixture in the W-P⁴⁵ kind of text is not simple to describe. There is evidence of some "Western" influence in its readings. There is even clearer evidence of textual *tendencies* that are especially identified with texts apparently made for popular consumption. These tendencies led (1) to the formation

---

[4]The expression τὸ πνεῦμα τὸ ἀκάθαρτον, with or without the articles and in singular or plural form, occurs eleven times in Mark, one time in Matthew, and five times in Luke (Moulton-Geden 819-20).

of "easier," "clearer" readings, and (2) to frequent harmonization of phrases with parallels in the other Gospels. The lack of the severe rearrangements of text and the lack of the freer paraphrasing in W and P[45], such as found in D, seem to indicate that the direct influence of the Western text upon the text of W and P[45] was somewhat muted.[5]

In the places where P[45] is extant, it is easy to see that the special agreements of W with P[45] show an "editorial" treatment of the text in Egypt. This editorial treatment means that the readings of P[45] and W are as much the result of scribal purposes as they are the result of any other force. Therefore, even if the theory concerning the development of the W-P[45] text put forth in this study is rejected (development from greater to lesser Neutral affinity), one cannot avoid the conclusion that, whatever the origins of the W-P[45] text, these witnesses are not a treasure trove of authentic Markan readings. In the next chapter we will examine more complete information on the kind of "editorial" activity that affected these Egyptian MSS.

[5]Colwell has called for a renewed study of the actual relationship of P[45] and Codex D; he questioned Kenyon's views about extensive Western influence upon the text of P[45] (*Studies in Methodology* 124). See also Hills's criticism of Kenyon on the same score ("The Caesarean Family of New Testament Manuscripts," 59-60).

CHAPTER VI

SCRIBAL PURPOSES OF CODEX W

IMPORTANCE OF SINGULAR READINGS

In the study of Greek MSS of the NT, emphasis is usually placed upon the readings which show some agreement with other witnesses. The singular readings (readings found in only one MS) are often set aside as of little importance. They are, of course, usually meaningless in determining the agreement and relationship of a textual witness with other witnesses. Further, it is unlikely that a reading found in only one MS is an original reading. Such a singular reading is probably a scribal creation—either accidental or deliberate. Yet singular readings are of definite importance in the overall task of textual criticism.

First, a textual critic's knowledge of singular readings can be of help in evaluating all readings on the basis of what is called internal evidence of readings. Hort wrote:

> Internal Evidence of Readings is of two kinds, which cannot be too sharply distinguished from each other; appealing respectively to Intrinsic Probability, having reference to the author, and what may be called Transcriptional Probability, having reference to the Copyists. In appealing to the first, we ask what an author is likely to have written: in appealing to the second, we ask what copyists are likely to have made him seem to write.[1]

In order to make judgments about such matters, the text critic needs to know just what kinds of changes scribes actually made in their copies. Without such knowledge, any conjecture about how alternative readings may have developed and about which variant is more likely to be the original reading must be termed untutored guesswork.

Second, in weighing the significance of agreements, how does one determine whether an agreement is really an indication of a genealogical relationship? Is it really true that "identity of reading implies identity of origin"?[2] How great a role did independent but coincidental scribal changes play in producing similar readings? To answer these questions one must have some data on how various scribes did their work and how free they felt to make what they considered to be improvements. All text critics are aware of the general kinds of intentional and unintentional changes evidenced in MSS of the Greek NT.[3] What is needed is solid

---

[1]B. F. Westcott and F. J. A. Hort, *The New Testament in the Original Greek: Introduction* 19-20.

[2]Ibid., 46. Hort's complete statement shows an awareness that the above-quoted statement is overly simplistic: "strictly speaking it implies either identity of origin or accidental coincidence. . . ."

[3]A handy description of the basic categories of all such changes can be found in B. M. Metzger, *The Text of the New Testament* 186-206.

study of important MSS to determine the habits and purposes of their scribes so that precise knowledge might be made available for answers to the questions posed above.[4]

In the previous chapters of this study, when agreements were examined, we made frequent reference to the relative insignificance of agreements in minor harmonizations as well as in common improvements of Markan style. This chapter will provide further justification for this line of reasoning. The basic point of this chapter will be that Codex Washingtonianus in Mark demonstrates the work of a scribe who independently created readings in his text—readings with reasonably clear editorial purposes. Therefore, when W agrees with another MS in readings which reflect such editorial purposes, these agreements should be used only with caution as evidence of genetic relationship. The obvious reasoning behind this caution is that if the scribe of W could make editorial changes in his text, it is very likely that other scribes did so also. Agreements in readings that appear to be such editorial changes are significant only when there is a generally high quantitative agreement in the total text of the two MSS being considered.[5]

This chapter will deal only with intentional changes in Codex W. Unintentional changes, spelling habits, and the like would prove nothing one way or the other concerning the tendency of scribes to make editorial changes.

It is sometimes difficult to determine whether a variant has been created intentionally or unintentionally. In the following discussion of readings, we will note when there is some chance that a reading might have been caused accidentally. As a basic working principle, we may say that when a variant cannot be attributed to the common scribal mistakes in copying, and especially when the variant can be attributed to a reasonable editorial intention, it is very likely that the variant is an intentional change.

There is an adequate treatment of the unintentional variants in Codex W in Sanders's collation.[6] According to Sanders's analysis, the scribe of W was generally a careful worker. There are extremely few nonsense readings or other indications of careless copying. This characterization of the scribe accords well with the thesis defended here concerning the intentional changes found in the MS— *Codex W shows conscious care to "improve" the sense of the text of Mark.*

In the face of the multitude of Greek witnesses (many of which have never been collated), the gathering of a list of truly "singular" readings seems practically impossible. Therefore, in this study singular readings are those for which no support could be found in Tischendorf's 8th edition[7] or in Legg's apparatus.[8] This is, admittedly, not an infallible method of insuring that every single variant cited here

---

[4]See what is probably a "pioneering" work in this type of study (at least for the Greek NT) by E. C. Colwell, "Scribal Habits in Early Papyri: A Study in the Corruption of the Text," *The Bible in Modern Scholarship* (ed. J. Philip Hyatt; Nashville: Abingdon, 1965) 370-89 (repr. as "Method in Evaluating Scribal Habits," *Studies in Methodology* 106-24). Note also Gordon D. Fee, *Papyrus Bodmer II (P66): Its Textual Relationships and Scribal Characteristics.*

[5]This advice has the support of Colwell, *Studies in Methodology* 107.

[6]Henry A. Sanders, *The New Testament Manuscripts in the Freer Collection* 4-40.

[7]Constantinus Tischendorf, *Novum Testamentum graece* (8th ed., 1869) I.

[8]S. C. E. Legg, *Novum Testamentum Graece: Euangelium secundum Marcum* (Oxford: Clarendon, 1935).

is really a singular variant. The conclusions of this chapter do not, however, depend upon a few examples.[9]

It is assumed that readings without support from other MSS are due to the individual purposes of the scribe of W. Codex W no doubt contains many more intentional variants than the ones listed here. As stated above, many of the agreements of Codex W with other witnesses in readings reflecting obvious editorial purposes are probably coincidental agreements. Proof for these statements, however, must be gathered from demonstrating the intentional editorial changes typical of Codex W, and this demonstration can be done best with readings peculiar to W.

While scholars may differ concerning the exact cause of a few variants discussed here, the conclusions of this chapter remain unshaken, for the examples are numerous for each category of editorial purposes. It should be noted that it is not absolutely essential that the variants mentioned here must be the work of the particular scribe of W. It is theoretically possible that some of the variants were created earlier than Codex W and that the scribe of Codex W copied faithfully his exemplar. Colwell has demonstrated that P[45], a much earlier MS, shows deliberate editorial changes similar to those discussed here.[10] If the changes studied in this chapter are not the work of the scribe of W, they are still evidence that deliberate and independent changes were made in the textual tradition of Mark represented by Codex W. That is, whether the copyist of Codex W or another, earlier copyist made the changes, they were still intentional changes apparently created with clear editorial purposes in view. The conclusions that such deliberate changes were probably made by other scribes and that agreements in such readings are coincidental would stand whether the particular scribe of Codex W or an earlier copyist made the changes here offered as evidence.

The singular readings of Codex W are classified below into some basic categories which have been conceived inductively from a study of these variants.

HARMONIZATIONS

Under this category we list a number of singular readings in the Markan text of W that were probably derived from parallel passages in the other Gospels. Some of the readings under this heading might not have been conscious harmonizations; they may have been created simply because the scribe felt that alterations were needed. But whenever in this study there seemed any chance that a reading might have been introduced into the Markan text of W from the other Gospels, the reading has been listed here. The other categories contain readings that cannot be attributed to har-

---

[9]A similar, though less rigorous method was used by Colwell in "Method in Evaluating Scribal Habits," *Studies in Methodology* 108-9. It was less rigorous in that he consulted only the apparatus of Tischendorf's 8th edition, attempting to take account of textual evidence since Tischendorf by checking important collations. Also, Colwell excluded only readings with support by other Greek MSS, while in this study readings were omitted with any Greek or versional support listed in the works consulted.

[10]Ibid., 118-21, 123-24. Burkitt was convinced that the unique readings in W were made in stages, and that only a few were made by the actual scribe of W. His views may be correct, but as he himself shows, this does not invalidate the basic thesis which he and the present writer defend ("W and Θ," 7).

monization. Those readings are results of a freer editing of the Markan text that led to the "creation" of really "new" readings.

The harmonizations listed below show that one scribal tendency in Codex W is to harmonize Mark with passages in the other Gospels. This being so, agreements of Codex W with other MSS in harmonistic readings can demonstrate only a common scribal tendency.

Mark 1:10b. W reads here . . . πνεῦμα καταβαῖνον ἀπὸ τοῦ οὐρανοῦ ὡσεί περιστερὰν καὶ μένον ἐπ'αὐτόν. It will be seen that the full construction of W in this verse does not derive from any of the Gospel parallels (Matt 3:16; Luke 3:21f.; John 1:32) word for word.

Mark 1:15. W has βασιλεία τῶν οὐρανῶν for βασιλεία τοῦ Θεοῦ. The former phrase is borrowed from the Matt 4:16 parallel.

Mark 1:24. W adds ὧδε before οἶδα. This may show familiarity with the D text of Luke 4:34, which also contains the word.

Mark 1:39. W omits καὶ τὰ δαιμόνια ἐκβάλλων. This omission may have been prompted by the lack of mention of this activity in the Matt 4:23 and Luke 4:44 parallels. There is, however, another interesting omission of the reference to exorcism in W in Mark 1:32, where W is supported by the Sinaitic Syr.

Mark 2:15. The choice of ἀνακειμένων αὐτῶν for κατακεῖσθαι αὐτόν might have been partly influenced by the Matt 9:10 parallel.

Mark 2:17. W reads ἐλήλυθα for the aorist form. This may be a scribal "improvement" or it may be a change conditioned by the more familiar Luke 5:32 parallel which uses the perfect form.

Mark 3:14. Here W adds μαθητάς after δώδεκα. This is a possible harmonization with the Matt 5:1 and Luke 6:13 parallels.

Mark 3:18-19. In the list of apostles W seems to be very close to the Luke 6:14-16 parallel. It should be noted that W mentions only eleven men, excluding altogether any mention of Mark's Thaddeus. W has not replaced him with the Judas son of James mentioned in the Lukan account.

Mark 3:34. The most different item in the verse in W is the addition of τοὺς μαθητάς after καθημένους. While this may be simply an independent clarification, it is possibly a clarification based on the presence of τοὺς μαθητάς in the Matt 12:49 parallel.[11]

Mark 4:32. It is possible that the scribe of W simply preferred a clearer word to describe the growth of plants—αὔξει for ἀναβαίνει,[12] but it is equally possible that the variant was in fact prompted by the preference for the former verb in the Matt 13:32 and Luke 13:19 parallels.

Mark 7:19. W here prefers χωρεῖ over ἐκπορεύεται, probably because of the presence of the former word in the Matt 15:17 parallel.

Mark 10:35. Here there is a preference for the verb προσέρχομαι over προσπορεύομαι, no doubt based on the use of the former word in the Matt 20:20 parallel.

Mark 11:31. W adds ὅτι after λέγοντες. This same construction appears

---

[11]F. C. Burkitt argued that this change was in fact an independent change and not a harmonization ("W and Θ," 6-7).
[12]Cf. ibid., 5-6.

in the Luke 20:5 parallel. It is questionable whether this really is a harmonization, but since a parallel can be found the variant is listed under this category.

Mark 14:41. W has καί for ἰδού before παραδίδοται. This may be prompted by the more familiar parallel in Matt 26:45, which has the former construction.

It is easy to see that the readings of W here classed as harmonizations are usually small variants. They invariably serve to improve or clarify the Markan text. The harmonist whose work is seen in W did not slavishly harmonize his work with the other Gospels, but used the familiar wording of the more popular Gospels to resolve Markan ambiguities or other Markan expressions he judged to be poor. It is hardly possible that this scribe was the only one who worked with these purposes. Therefore, agreements of Codex W with other MSS precisely in these kinds of harmonizations mean little for textual relationships without overall agreement in a majority of all readings.

VOCABULARY PREFERENCES

Here we note what appear to be examples of preferences for words and expressions that apparently reflect the personal tastes of the scribe. The changes cannot be accounted for by assuming that they are direct harmonizations; there are no such variants in the parallel passages in the other Gospels.

Mark 1:27. W prefers ἐθαύμαζον here over ἐθαμβήθησαν in describing the crowd's response to Jesus' teaching. The same word is preferred again in W in Mark 2:12 where W has ὥστε θαυμάζειν αὐτούς for ὥστε ἐξιστάσθαι πάντας.

Mark 2:3. W prefers βαστάζοντες over φέροντες in describing the carrying of the lame man.

Mark 2:4. W reads προσελθεῖν instead of προσενέγκαι (ℵ, B) or προσεγγίσαι (TR, A).

Mark 2:4. W reads εἰς ὅν for ὅπου.

Mark 2:19. The phrase υἱοὶ τοῦ νυμφῶνος appears in W as νυμφίοι τοῦ νυμφῶνος. The former reading must have appeared puzzling or awkward to a person unfamiliar with Semitic expressions, and so a clearer phrase was substituted.

Mark 2:21. W here has πλείω σχίσμα in place of χεῖρον σχίσμα.

Mark 3:11. W has ἴδον instead of ἐθεώρουν.

Mark 4:1. Here W reads παρὰ τὸν αἰγιαλόν for παρὰ τὴν θάλασσαν.

Mark 4:4. W substitutes ὄρνεα for πετεινὰ τοῦ οὐρανοῦ.

Mark 4:5. W substitutes ἀνέτειλε for ἐξανέτειλε, which the scribe may have felt to be too cumbersome a word.

Mark 4:22. W reads here οὐδὲν γὰρ ἐστίν for οὐ γάρ ἐστίν τι, which also may have seemed an awkward expression in need of polishing.

Mark 4:37. Here W uses εἰσέβαλλεν rather than ἐπέβαλλεν to describe the waves swamping the boat. The former compound verb agrees with the following prepositional phrase in the context—εἰς τὸ πλοῖον.

Mark 5:31. The term συνθλίβοντα is exchanged for συντρίβοντα to describe the pressing crowd.

Mark 6:13. W uses ἐξέπεμπον rather than ἐξέβαλλον to describe the exorcisms.

Mark 6:31. There is the change here from ὀλίγον to λοιπόν in W.

Mark 7:6. W has the simple form ἔχει for ἀπέχει.

Mark 7:10. In the commandment against abusing one's parents, W has ἀθετῶν rather than κακολογῶν.

Mark 7:19. W's use here of διάνοιαν for καρδίαν perhaps indicates some objection to the use of the figurative term.[13]

Mark 7:33. W reads προσλαβόμενος for ἀπολαβόμενος to describe Jesus' taking aside of a man to be healed.

Mark 9:45. There is another preference for a simple verb form—κόψον for ἀπόκοψον.

Mark 10:7. W has ἕκαστος rather than ἄνθρωπος in the citation of the Gen 2:24 passage.

Mark 10:22. W prefers to say that the young man went away sad ἀπὸ τοῦ λόγου rather than ἐπὶ τῷ λόγῳ.

Mark 11:2. W uses ᾧ rather than ἐφ' ὅν, and, in the same verse, W reads ἐπικεκάθεικεν for ἐκάθισεν (א, B, Θ, 565) or κεκάθικεν (TR, A).

Mark 11:12. Here W prefers αὔριον for ἐπαύριον.

Mark 11:29. W reads τίνι for ποίᾳ.

Mark 12:1. Again, W has a compound verb form for the simple form— ἐξώρυξεν for ὤρυξεν.

Mark 13:2. W rewords the whole latter part of this verse, but here one need note only the preference of διαλυθήσεται for καταλυθήσεται (א, Θ, Fam 13) or καταλυθῇ (TR, A, B, D).

Mark 13:9. W has the simple form δώσουσιν for παραδώσουσιν.

Mark 14:27. Again, W prefers the simple verb σκορπισθήσεται over the compound διασκορπισθήσεται.

Mark 14:32. W has the reading ἐξέρχονται for ἔρχονται. The scribe may have wanted to make clear that the group went out from the room of the supper to Gethsemane.

Mark 16:1. W prefers a compound form here—εἰσελθοῦσαι rather than ἐλθοῦσαι—perhaps to make clear that the women would have to *enter* the tomb to anoint Jesus' body.

Mark 16:5. Here W reads θεωροῦσιν for εἶδον. Compare this example with the opposite preference in Mark 3:11 cited above.

Surely it is clear that W shows evidence of an individual attempt to clarify the text by the substitution of words at various places in the Markan text. The scribe responsible for this activity felt an apparent freedom to substitute simple for compound verbs and compound for simple. It seems that changes in words sometimes were influenced by the mere verbal tastes of the scribe. In other cases, the change was a more logical one designed to fit the sense of the context. The only consistent word preference noted was the use of θαυμάζω twice to describe the reaction of people to Jesus.

Colwell's study of scribal changes in P⁴⁵, P⁶⁶, and P⁷⁵ showed similar

[13]The source for this change may be in Mark 12:28, where καρδίαν and διάνοιαν are used together to represent the OT word לֵבָב.

concern for stylistic improvement, especially in P[45]. This concern led to "clarifications" of various kinds including substitution of verb forms and synonyms. The data reinforce the idea that such free changes were common among many scribes.[14]

GRAMMATICAL IMPROVEMENTS

Here follows a list of cases where W shows readings that appear to be deliberate improvements in grammatical construction. Most of the changes appear to be the small changes a high school composition teacher might make in a pupil's paper work.

Mark 1:6. W has ἦν before the participle ἐσθίων. Without ἦν the participle seems to dangle in that it is separated considerably from the nearest auxiliary verb.

Mark 1:9. W adds καί before ἦλθεν, perhaps in an attempt to smooth over the asyndeton.

Mark 2:26. Here W reads εἰσελθών rather than εἰσῆλθεν in another attempt to smooth out a usage of two finite verbs without conjunction.

Mark 3:5. Where other MSS have καὶ περιβλεψάμενος, W reads περιβλεψάμενος δέ. The reason for this variant is that there is a change of subject in the context.

Mark 3:10. W uses ἐπίπιπτον in place of the infinitive ἐπιπίπτειν in a result clause. The preference may show Attic tastes in the scribe of W.[15]

Mark 3:11. Here there is another preference for δέ rather than καί because there is a change of subject. W reads τὰ πνεύματα δέ rather than καὶ τὰ πνεύματα.

Mark 3:22. W has οἱ ἀπὸ Ἱεροσολύμων καταβάντες γραμματεῖς instead of οἱ γραμματεῖς οἱ ἀπὸ Ἱεροσολύμων καταβάντες. W prefers this more simplified attributive position of the article.

Mark 4:16. W uses οἵτινες for οἱ, perhaps because the scribe felt that the latter did not serve well for the relative pronoun.

Mark 4:17. A change that is far less clearly an improvement is the addition in W of καί before εὐθύς. The absence of καί does not leave the phrase awkward, but the scribe preferred the sound of the phrase with the conjunction. Sometimes his personal tastes are not easily explained.

Mark 4:18. Again W adds δέ. Here it is after ἄλλοι εἰσὶν οἱ, and again it seems to be added to indicate a contrast between the items being mentioned.

Mark 5:4. W has μηδένα δέ for καὶ οὐδείς because there is a change of subject.

Mark 6:45. W reads ἕως ἂν αὐτὸς ἀπολύσῃ for ἕως αὐτὸς ἀπολύει. The indefiniteness of the statement no doubt seemed to the scribe to demand the proper subjunctive construction.

Mark 8:5. This is another example of W preferring δέ over καί in the opening phrase of the verse. By now it is very clear that this is one of the scribe's more pronounced preferences.

[14]E. C. Colwell, *Studies in Methodology* 119-23.
[15]See BDF §391.

Mark 14:13. W rejects the paratactic καὶ ἀποστέλλει . . . καὶ λέγει in favor of the less colloquial καὶ ἀποστείλας . . . λέγει.

In addition to these examples we may note some changes in tense and voice of verbs.

Mark 5:19—ἠλέηκεν for ἠλέησεν.
Mark 6:20—ἠπορεῖτο for ἠπόρει (ℵ, B, Θ). (TR, A, D, 565, and Fam 13 read ἐποίει.)
Mark 7:13—παρέδοτε for παρεδώκατε.
Mark 9:31—λέγει for ἔλεγεν.
Mark 10:35—αἰτησώμεθα for αἰτήσωμεν.
Mark 12:10—ἀνεγνώκατε for ἀνέγνωτε.
Mark 16:8—ἔσχεν for εἶχεν.

However clear or obscure the reasons may be today for such changes, the fact is that they were made because a scribe felt that they would be helpful in rendering a passage easier to read and to understand. The only possible exception is the change in 9:31, which substitutes a historic present verb form for an aorist form. This list of minor changes in verb tense and voice adds to the stock of evidence that the text of W represents a fairly thorough and independent editorial treatment of the Gospel of Mark. When W agrees with other MSS in such changes as those given above, the agreement must not be given much significance.

CHANGES TOWARD CONCISE EXPRESSION

The variants listed here generally consist of omissions of words or phrases. The result is a more concise text that sacrifices nothing meaningful. In some cases the variant is a substitution but with the same interest in concise expression.

Mark 1:37. W omits καὶ εὗρον αὐτόν (ℵ, B) or καὶ εὑρόντες αὐτόν (TR, A, Θ, 565, Fam 13). It is stated in the context that the disciples went after Jesus and that they spoke to him, so it is obvious that they found him.

Mark 2:16. W omits ἰδόντες ὅτι ἐσθίει μετὰ τῶν ἁμαρτωλῶν καὶ τελωνῶν (ℵ, B). It is possible that this could be regarded as a harmonization in that the Matt 9:11 parallel omits this phrase as well. It appears, however, that the omission in the Markan text of W may just as easily have been prompted by a feeling that the inclusion of the phrase made a repetitious passage, for practically the same words occur next in the verse on the lips of Jesus' accusers.

Mark 3:4. Here W has ἀγαθὸν ποιῆσαι ἢ οὔ while others read κακοποιῆσαι for the last word of the phrase. The expression in W is clear and more concise.

Mark 3:25. W omits ἡ οἰκία ἐκείνη, no doubt because it was considered needlessly wordy. It is clear what the subject of δυνήσεται στῆναι is without the omitted words.

Mark 4:4. W omits ἐγένετο ἐν τῷ σπείρειν, which was also seen as needless verbiage in the light of the preceding statement, ἐξῆλθεν ὁ σπείρων σπεῖραι.

Mark 4:5. The phrase διὰ τὸ μὴ ἔχειν βάθος γῆς is omitted in W. The preceding statement makes mention of the shallow ground, and the words omitted were probably seen as a redundancy.

Mark 5:31. W omits αὐτοῦ after οἱ μαθηταί for the same reason. The article itself indicates sufficiently whose disciples were intended.

Mark 5:40. W changes τοὺς μετ᾿ αὐτοῦ to τοὺς ἑαυτοῦ, not an omission, but a more concise phrase.

Mark 6:1. The phrase ἐκεῖθεν καὶ ἔρχεται (ℵ, B, Θ) is omitted in W. The resultant text reads καὶ ἐξῆλθεν εἰς τὴν πατρίδα αὐτοῦ, a clear and less wordy phrase.

Mark 6:10. Here W drops αὐτοῖς after ἔλεγεν. Those addressed have already been mentioned in 6:8, and the omitted indirect object is therefore unnecessary.

Mark 7:13. W omits καὶ παρόμοια τοιαῦτα πολλὰ ποιεῖτε. Sanders regarded this as an accidental omission due to the similarity of the ending of the last word in the phrase and the ending of παρεδώκατε, which precedes this phrase.[16] This is possible, but such homoioteleutons are not frequent in W, by Sanders's own admission, while conscious omissions are. The phrase in question may easily have been seen as a needless generalizing phrase that could well be omitted. It is interesting that with the phrase omitted the text shows no sign of discontinuity. While it is not impossible for a sense unit to be omitted accidentally, this example more easily fits the modus operandi of the scribe, who deliberately deleted what he considered wordy phrases.

Mark 8:6. Here W reads αὐτοῖς in place of τοῖς μαθηταῖς αὐτοῦ. The identity of αὐτοῖς is perfectly clear, and the substitution makes the text less wordy.

Mark 8:29. W similarly drops the last word from the phrase τίνα με λέγετε εἶναι, leaving a clear but shorter phrase.

Mark 9:28. W omits the pronoun in the expression οἱ μαθηταί αὐτοῦ, and leaves the article to identify the disciples.

Mark 10:21. Here W omits ὁ δέ at the beginning of the verse, although there is a change of speaker and the words omitted would serve to indicate this change of speaker in good grammatical form. Perhaps the scribe omitted the words to remove the repetition of the phrase, which is found four times in the immediate context.

Mark 10:28. W reads πάντα ἀφήκαμεν for ἰδοὺ ἡμεῖς ἀφήκαμεν πάντα and thus creates another concise statement.

Mark 10:39. W omits ὁ δὲ Ἰησοῦς εἶπεν αὐτοῖς. This omission seems to go beyond a desire for conciseness and leaves a rather abrupt text in this verse.

Mark 10:46. W drops Βαρτιμαῖος perhaps because υἱὸς Τιμαίου was deemed sufficient identification.

Mark 11:15. W omits καὶ (τοὺς) ἀγοράζοντας (ℵ, B, A), an omission which Sanders again attributed to homoioteleuton.[17] While this is a possible explanation, it is just as possible that the scribe felt that τοὺς πωλοῦντας which precedes the omitted phrase was a sufficient description of the recipients of Jesus' censure. This omission is clearly the weakest example given in this list. It need not be pressed, for there are plenty of other examples of deliberate omissions.

Mark 12:2. The phrase πρὸς τοὺς γεωργούς is omitted in W no doubt

---

[16]Sanders, *The New Testament Manuscripts in the Freer Collection* 26.
[17]Ibid.

because these workers are mentioned again in the next phrase. With the omission the text is perfectly smooth and concise.

Mark 12:5. W omits κἀκεῖνον ἀπέκτειναν. The phrase can be taken as interrupting an otherwise fairly smooth narrative which tells of the collective treatment of the landowner's messengers.

Mark 12:21. W omits καί twice: once before ὁ δεύτερος, and again before ὁ τρίτος. Perhaps this is an attempt to break the monotony of connectives used here.

Mark 12:44. W drops πάντα ὅσα εἶχεν because the phrase that follows, ὅλον τὸν βιόν αὐτῆς, is plainly sufficient to describe the woman's sacrifice.

Mark 14:22. W removes the last word from the genitive absolute καὶ ἐσθιόντων αὐτῶν. If this is the result of a desire for concise expression, it is an example of the rather strong tastes of the scribe.

Mark 14:30. W drops the last word from the phrase ἀμὴν λέγω σοι. Again this seems to be evidence of a desire to drop a pronoun whenever it was expendable.

Mark 14:60. W omits οὐκ ἀποκρίνῃ οὐδέν, the reason perhaps being that the next verse says ὁ δὲ ἐσιώπα. The former phrase may have seemed needless.

While a couple of these examples could be attributed to accidental omission, the bulk of these cases indicates a pattern of omitting phrases when the scribe felt that they were needless and wordy. The result of his work is almost invariably a clear, meaningful text that is also shorter and often smoother. The agreement of Codex W with another MS in this kind of variant is not in itself of much significance, for W shows that such readings were often consciously and independently created by scribes.

ADDITIONS FOR CLARIFICATION

The following examples are cases wherein the desire for clarity prompted a longer reading. This indicates that the scribe's fondness for a concise (and generally shorter) text was balanced by a willingness to add to the text in order to clarify it.

Mark 2:22. W adds ἀλλ᾽εἰς καινούς after παλαιούς. The added words specify the contrast implied in their absence.

Mark 5:37. W has μόνον after εἰ μή to make clear that *only* Peter, James, and John accompanied Jesus.

Mark 8:3. Here W adds ἕως before εἰς οἶκον. The addition makes it clear that the crowds would have to go hungry until they reached their homes if Jesus sent them away.

Mark 8:5. W adds ὧδε after πόσους, specifying that Jesus asked only how many loaves the disciples had *immediately at hand* without locating others.

Mark 9:42. W inserts μου after τῶν μικρῶν to emphasize that the reference is to Jesus' disciples and not to children.

Mark 10:22. W has ἀπ᾽αὐτοῦ after ἀπῆλθεν. The addition frankly seems unnecessary, but the scribe must have felt it helpful to emphasize that it was a departure *away* from Jesus.

Mark 12:41. Here W adds πάντας after ἐθεώρει. Again the addition does not seem quite necessary but must have appeared so to the scribe.

Mark 14:23. W reads τοῖς μαθηταῖς in place of αὐτοῖς to make it clear that Jesus gave the cup to the *disciples*. Further, in the context the third person plural pronoun is used repeatedly, and the scribe may have felt it well to break the monotony.

Mark 14:28. W adds ἐκ νεκρῶν after ἐγερθῆναι, obviously in an attempt to make explicit the reference to the resurrection of Jesus.

Mark 15:46. Here W has εὐθέως ἤνεγκεν after σινδόνα. This simply makes explicit that Joseph brought the burial clothes to the place of burial.

Two more examples will suffice to show how the scribe of W could either add or omit the article in individual cases as he saw fit. In 13:17 W drops ταῖς before θηλαζούσαις; but in 12:38 W adds ταῖς before στολαῖς, without obvious reason in either case.

This list shows that the scribe of W could add as well as omit, although the number of additions is noticeably less than the number of omissions. It is clear that the scribe generally preferred a concise reading. None of his additions is a redundancy, and each one seems to be an attempt to make the particular statements in question more explicit. If some of the additions do not appear to the modern student as necessary, that only shows that the editorial changes were dictated by personal taste, thus reinforcing the point being made here that scribes consciously created readings of this kind.

SIGNIFICANT SENSE CHANGES[18]

The variants listed in this section are readings which make a noticeable alteration in the sense of the statement. These changes appear to affect the content of the passage and not merely the style.

Mark 3:3. W has Jesus command the man with the withered hand to stand ἐκ τοῦ μέσου in place of εἰς τὸ μέσον. Perhaps this implies that the scribe thought Jesus was telling the man to stand apart from the more hostile group gathered in the synagogue.

Mark 3:21. Here is one of the more significant changes in W. In place of the Neutral reading ἐξέστη, or the D reading ἐξέσταται αὐτούς, W reads ἐξήρτηνται αὐτοῦ. There are several other alternative readings in various MSS, some of which are practically meaningless. The reading of the Neutrals is clear; the charge is, "He is mad." The reading of W is equally clear and obviously a deliberate change—"They are his adherents."[19] There can be no doubt that here a scribe has removed an objectionable statement that struck at his Christology. In its place he has put an inoffensive statement which has some slight phonetic similarity to the other variants. This similarity possibly shows that the scribe believed himself to be "correcting" a mistaken reading—perhaps what he regarded as a misspelling in the exemplar before him.

---

[18]This study does not make reference to the famous Freer Logion, which is the ending to Mark found only in Codex W among Greek MSS. The most complete treatment of this variant is by Caspar R. Gregory, *Das Freer-Logion* (Leipzig: J. C. Hinrich, 1908). See also, more recently, W. L. Lane, *The Gospel According to Mark* (NICNT; Grand Rapids: Eerdmans, 1974) 606-11.

[19]See the comments of O. Linton, "Evidences of a Second-Century Revised Edition of St. Mark's Gospel," *NTS* 14(1968) 330. Also note F. C. Burkitt, "W and Θ," 10-12.

Mark 6:5. W reads οὐκέτι rather than ἐκεῖ, making the sentence read, "He was *no longer* able to work a miracle," rather than, "He was not able *there* to work a miracle." There does not seem to be any significant weakening of the idea that Jesus found himself unable to work a miracle. Perhaps, in the scribe's mind, his change smoothed out the difficulty found in the Neutral text reading, which states that Jesus was unable to work a miracle and then mentions the healing of a few sick people. That is, perhaps the reading is intended to say that after these healings Jesus was unable to work a miracle—"any longer."

Mark 6:8. The usual text gives a command not to take money on the missionary trip εἰς τὴν ζώνην. W changes the last word to πήραν. The latter word is found in the context, and its place here may be due to the scribal failure to understand how money could be carried in a "belt." He therefore substituted the usual word, "wallet," which lay at hand in the passage.

Mark 6:11. The command here is for the preachers to shake the dust off their sandals in an unfriendly town εἰς μαρτύριον αὐτοῖς. W reads αὐτῶν for the last word and makes the phrase apparently mean "a testimony concerning them" rather than "a testimony against them."

Mark 8:14. The word ἐπελάθοντο is omitted in favor of ἀπέλθοντες. The Matt 16:5 parallel has ἐλθόντες but also mentions that the disciples forgot to take bread with them. The reading in W cannot be a simple harmonization. For some reason the scribe may have found the forgetfulness of the disciples objectionable.

Mark 9:24. In this case there is a most interesting variant. W changes ὁ πατὴρ τοῦ παιδίου to τὸ πνεῦμα τοῦ παιδαρίου. There are really two changes here. The one is a minor preference for the term which indicates a somewhat older child. More striking is the substitution of "spirit" for "father." Perhaps the scribe felt that the anguished cry seemed more likely to have come from the troubled boy. The scribe may have thought that the "father" was an unintentional error and that the proper word had to be inserted into the text.

Mark 9:20. W omits the pronoun from the phrase which states that upon seeing Jesus the unclean spirit ἐσπάραξεν αὐτόν. The reason seems to be that αὐτόν is used twice in the immediately preceding sentence with reference to Jesus. In the phrase in question the pronoun no doubt represents the demoniac boy. To avoid confusion in the mind of the reader W simply omits the ambiguous pronoun.

Mark 9:49. Here is a sentence that has several alternative textual forms. The one found in the Neutral tradition is πᾶς γὰρ πυρὶ ἁλισθήσεται. This is an obviously obscure statement which W changes by making the last word ἁλισγηθήσεται! The obscure reference about being "salted" with fire is now made to read "polluted" with fire. In the context of the description of Gehenna this "correction" obviously refers to future judgment. The variant of W is not an accidental misspelling but a thoughtful attempt to make the dark saying meaningful to the reader by the use of the contextual thought. The variant in W might even be called a "midrashic" or interpretative treatment of the text.[20]

Mark 10:32. W omits ἐφοβοῦντο perhaps because no such mention of the disciples' attitude is made in the Synoptic parallels. It is also possible that the

[20]Burkitt, "W and Θ," 16-18. "The variants in this verse show clearly that not palaeographical error but arbitrary conjectural emendation is the main parent of the 'various readings' in our MSS" (17-18).

scribe found the mention of the disciples' fear meaningless or even objectionable. There is nothing frightening mentioned in the context, only the trip to Jerusalem. The scribe perhaps felt that the mention of amazement on the part of the disciples was an understandable and proper attitude in Jesus' presence but that fear was not acceptable.

Mark 10:38. After the request of James and John for seats of honor in Jesus' kingdom, Jesus replies to them with a question that seems to envision their violent death. It is interesting that W changes the phrase which introduces the prophetic question from Ἰησοῦς εἶπεν αὐτοῖς to Ἰησοῦς ἀποκριθεὶς εἶπεν αὐτῷ. This is a minor change, but it does possibly reflect familiarity with church tradition, which held that only James suffered martyrdom while John lived to old age.

Mark 12:12. The generally supported reading mentions the enemies of Jesus being incensed over the parable of the vineyard. Then follows καὶ ἀφέντες αὐτὸν ἀπῆλθον. W omits this sentence apparently because in the next verse Jesus' enemies are still present, testing him with provocative questions. The scribe must have thought that the statement in question was confusing to the reader and so dropped it. The resultant text is quite sensible.

Mark 12:26. Here W changes ὅτι to εἰ to make the text read "as to *whether* the dead are raised" rather than "as to the dead, *that* they are raised." This seems to be a rephrasing of the text to make it more easily understood.

Mark 12:29. The generally supported reading gives Jesus' answer to the question about the chief command as κύριος ὁ θεὸς ἡμῶν κύριος εἷς ἔστιν. W drops εἷς, and the reason is possibly because calling God "one" seemed meaningless or perhaps at variance with the scribe's conception of the Trinity. The altered phrase reads in a "corrected" sense, "the Lord God is our Lord," or perhaps, "the Lord our God is Lord."

Mark 13:21. W reads ὁ κύριος for ὁ χριστός in the prophecy of eschatological deceivers. This surely indicates that at least in the circles of the scribe of W the term κύριος came to be the more familiar title for Jesus. The reading also seems to reflect a gentile church situation, while the dominant reading seems to reflect a Jewish-Christian setting in which "the Christ" would be much more a topic of discussion.

Mark 13:33. W inserts εἰ μὴ ὁ πατὴρ καὶ ὁ υἱός after οὐκ οἴδατε γάρ. This addition is out of character for the text of W, which generally has a more concise account. The variant occurs in a passage which says that no man knows the time of the end. The inserted words modify this statement to make it clear that the Father and Son do know the time. This is especially curious in that W preserves the usual text in Mark 13:32, which restricts this eschatological knowledge to the Father only. The addition here in 13:33 must be an attempt to soften the statement about Jesus' limited foreknowledge. The attempt is not well thought out, it seems, for the resultant text of W creates a contradiction between 13:32 and 13:33,[21] and the opening phrase of 13:33, as it appears in W, is somewhat awkward.

---

[21]It is interesting that in the Matt 24:36 parallel to Mark 13:32, W, with numerous other witnesses, omits οὐδὲ ὁ υἱός. This is all the more reason to wonder why the words were left *in* the *Markan* account. It is a glaring case of a passed-up opportunity to harmonize the Markan account with the Matthean account as it appears in W.

Mark 14:1. W changes the accomplices of the priests from γραμματεῖς to φαρισαῖοι. There seems to be no reason for this except that in the opinion of the scribe of W, the Pharisees were the real culprits and not the scribes.[22]

Mark 14:62. Here W changes τῶν νεφελῶν to τῆς δυνάμεως. Jesus thus promises the advent of the Son of man "seated at the right hand of the Power and coming with the *power* of Heaven." The reference to "clouds" must have seemed a puzzling expression to the scribe, and so again a meaningful word found in the context was substituted.

All of these examples show that the text of W gives evidence of a scribe who was not only interested in grammatical clarity, but who was also willing to make outright changes on the basis of his own ideas about proper content. He seems to have been interested in removing references to the fear or forgetfulness of the disciples. He could make doctrinal changes as in 3:21 or 13:33. He made readings more accommodating to ideas of the later church times as in 12:29; 13:21; 14:62; and probably 14:1 and 10:38. These more significant sense changes are few in proportion to the text as a whole, but they show that there was a greater degree of scribal freedom exercised in certain places and times than some have supposed.[23]

WORD ORDER

The following are examples of readings that are singular in word order. No clear pattern has been found governing the preferences of the scribe except that he seems to have preferred placing the possessive pronoun or genitive personal pronoun before the noun rather than after it. The cases are recorded here without comment on individual readings. They are not serious changes and are interesting only in that they show the scribe's interest even in such small details as word order. The variants are given with the reading of the Nestle text (25th edition) listed first and the reading of W following.

3:31	ἡ μήτηρ αὐτοῦ καὶ οἱ ἀδελφοὶ αὐτοῦ—αὐτοῦ ἡ μήτηρ καὶ οἱ ἀδελφοί.
4:32	ὑπὸ τὴν σκιὰν αὐτοῦ—αὐτοῦ ὑπὸ τὴν σκιάν.
5:3	οὐκέτι οὐδεὶς ἐδύνατο αὐτὸν δῆσαι—αὐτὸν οὐκέτι ἐδύνατο δῆσαι.
6:50	ἐγώ εἰμι, μὴ φοβεῖσθε—μὴ φοβεῖσθε, ἐγώ εἰμι.
8:12	τῇ γενεᾷ ταύτῃ—ταύτῃ τῇ γενεᾷ.
8:36	τὴν ψυχὴν αὐτοῦ—τὴν ἑαυτοῦ ψυχήν.
9:21	τὸν πατέρα αὐτοῦ—αὐτοῦ τὸν πατέρα.
12:23	τίνος αὐτῶν—αὐτῶν τίνος.
14:64	ὑμῖν φαίνεται—φαίνεται ὑμῖν.
15:4	πόσα σου κατηγοροῦσιν—σου πόσα κατηγοροῦσιν.
16:4	μέγας σφόδρα—σφόδρα μέγας.

[22]A reason for the scribe holding this opinion may be that throughout the Gospel of Mark, *except for the passion narrative,* the Pharisees are mentioned as active opponents of Jesus.

[23]See the study of dogmatic interest at work in the Western text of Acts by Eldon J. Epp, *The Theological Tendency of Codex Bezae Cantabrigiensis in Acts* (SNTSMS 3; Cambridge: Cambridge University, 1966). Epp refers to incorrect opinions about the possibility of dogmatic influence upon the textual transmission of the NT in pp. 1-3.

SUMMARY

The variants dealt with here total 134 cases where W has a singular reading that seems to be a deliberate change in the text. These, with only a few possible exceptions, are not "slips" but are changes made purposefully. As one examines these cases, the impression is inescapable that the text of W is the result of deliberate editorial activity.

Wherever it was possible, we have attempted to indicate the basic editorial purposes behind the particular readings. The scribe who made these changes knew Hellenistic Greek well. There does not seem to be much evidence of Attic Greek tendencies in his changes: the scribe had more personal and practical concerns than making Mark resemble some classical model. He was interested in producing a text of Mark that would be easy to read and as intelligible as possible. To accomplish this he "corrected" the style of Mark to that of more familiar Hellenistic Greek. Often he used the other Synoptic Gospels or the immediate context as a guide in vocabulary selection, but he had independent tastes too and could insert the word that he thought most appropriate. His dogmatic interests were restrained, but he was not above removing difficulties that might confuse the reader or that might challenge traditional ideas.

One must not place much emphasis upon agreements of W with other MSS in such matters as the use of δέ for καί, minor harmonizations, or even omissions of small units of text which might easily appear as redundant or wordy. The reason for this advice is that if the scribe of W made such independent changes in the text before him, then other scribes could have made similar changes independently, and agreements in such readings could be coincidental.

Thus, while W definitely does have a significant amount of agreement with Western witnesses, especially the OL MSS in Mark 1–4, some individual agreements of W with these, or with other witnesses, might be due to common editorial tendencies and not due to genetic relationship. Codex W and the Western witnesses do have a quantitative relationship in Mark 1–4 strong enough to justify the claim that there is some loose connection in this part of Mark (though the quantitative agreement is significantly below the level of agreement of primary witnesses of the same text-type such as א and B), but where the overall agreement of W with a MS is not very high, individual agreements in readings fitting the categories examined above cannot be pressed as evidence of a special relationship.

The text of W is not a "wild" text, if by that term one means an irresponsible treatment of the material transmitted. There was considerable scribal freedom exercised in the text represented by W, but that freedom was exercised with responsibility and with purpose. It is the freedom exercised by translators today who wish to free the text from outmoded or unfamiliar expressions. They therefore thoughtfully but unhesitatingly attempt to make the text more understandable in a new time and in a different tongue. Nearly all the scribal changes in Codex W seem prompted by a similar kind of concern to produce a copy of Mark in a style of Greek familiar to the reader of that day.

At this point we must pause to examine the theory of Olof Linton concerning a supposed early recension of Mark, since Linton's view is directly contrary to the views supported in this study. Linton believes that the various readings which appear to be deliberate improvements in Markan style are evidence

> that a revision of St. Mark's Gospel was carried out at a very early time, and that reminiscences of this revision are to be found in many manuscripts, amongst the Uncials particularly D, W and Θ, amongst the Cursives in the first place 565 and 700 but also many others, as for example Family 1 and Family 13, 28, 157 and 543, amongst the translations especially the Old Latin but often also the Syriac and others.[24]

Thirty pages of Professor Linton's thirty-five-page article look at specific variants to show that they are deliberate revisions of the original Markan reading. There is no quarrel here, and on this point Linton's work is helpful. He clearly appears to err, however, when he tries to explain these deliberate changes in all these witnesses as having come from a single revision. While it is highly likely that MSS which belong to the same textual group have inherited readings from a common ancestor, it is not likely that individual agreements between MSS that do not show close ties should be attributed to a common ancestor, especially when the agreements are variants that make minor improvements in the text. It is far more likely that similar or identical variants were produced independently by scribes with similar purposes and tastes.

Linton's idea concerning the origin of the deliberate-correction variants in Markan textual history cannot be accepted for several reasons.

First, many of his examples show *similar* readings, but not the *same* readings at the same place in the text of the witnesses reviewed. These similar-but-different readings are more likely the results of widespread scribal tendencies rather than a single revision effort.

Second, Linton has to admit that no MS or body of MSS preserves his "recension" reasonably intact. He is forced to "reconstruct" the readings of the hypothetical revision, usually by conflating readings from various witnesses. Thus, his only proof for this revision is the assumption that such a revision existed!

Third, Linton's list of witnesses to his supposed recension appears to be

---

[24] "Evidences of a Second-Century Revised Edition of St. Mark's Gospel," *NTS* 14(1968) 322. There have been other suggestions concerning early "recensions" of Mark, none of which has ever been successful in gaining acceptance. Thomas F. Glasson ("Did Matthew and Luke Use a 'Western' Text of Mark?" *Exp Tim* 55[1943/44] 180-84) suggested that Matthew and Luke used a "Western" text of Mark and that this accounts for the agreements of these two Gospels against Mark in many places. Pairman J. Brown ("An Early Revision of the Gospel of Mark," *JBL* 78[1959] 215-27) argued that in the first century there was a revision of Mark used by Matthew and Luke and that the revision was basically "Caesarean." T. F. Glasson ("An Early Revision of the Gospel of Mark," *JBL* 85[1966] 231-33) reviewed P. Brown's work and argued that Brown's "Caesarean" readings are really just typical "Western" readings. It appears that Glasson's analysis of the readings is more correct than Brown's and tends to support the analysis of the so-called Caesarean readings made in the present study. Both men err, however, in attempting to account for the many minor agreements of Matthew and Luke against Mark on the basis of some early revision of Mark. Neither scholar shows familiarity with the work of C. H. Turner ("Marcan Usage"), who cogently shows most Matthew-Luke agreements to be common stylistic improvements made by each Evangelist independently.

nothing more than a list of witnesses to the "Western text" of Mark. Linton has not produced evidence of an early, single revision of Mark, but has described, without recognizing it, the outlines of the "Western text" of Mark. It is hardly likely that the loose ties unifying this textual group stem from an early recension. Today it is clear that most textual groups are results of a process and not the remnants of individual "recensions."[25]

Fourth, Linton shows no awareness of the kind of evidence given in this chapter that scribes made deliberate and independent changes in their copies. Once this scribal activity is recognized, the scattered agreements of MSS in clear editorial changes can be put into proper perspective, a perspective that allows for many coincidental agreements of MSS to arise from common scribal tendencies.[26]

In short, Linton's theory is unnecessary to account for the evidence and shows a serious lack of awareness of the scribal treatment of the text of Mark.

CODEX W AND THE "CAESAREAN TEXT"

It is important now to relate the results of this chapter to the question of W's relationship to the "Caesarean text." In Chapter III of this study we noted that W and Θ do not have a high quantitative relationship with each other. We further noted that their individual agreements were very often the results of common possession of readings shared by many Western witnesses. Finally, it was noted that the W-Θ agreements not shared by important Western witnesses were nearly all readings which were obviously deliberate "improvements" in the Markan text. The copious examples furnished in this chapter of free scribal changes in Codex W reinforce the argument that many of those remaining W-Θ agreements were probably coincidental—the results of similar but independent scribal work.[27]

If Codex Θ is a good representative of the "Caesarean text," the poor and unexceptional agreement of Codex W with Θ makes it highly unlikely that W is related in any special way to this text-type. The doubts raised in Chapter III of this study seem to be confirmed by the results of this chapter.

THE NATURE OF THE W TEXT

All the readings investigated in this chapter are apparently singular readings of Codex W, and they enable us to see the nature of the W text apart from the effect of other textual influences upon the MS.

Ayuso, who erroneously described W and P[45] as early Caesarean witnesses, also erred in his description of the *quality* of text found in these MSS. Codex W does not represent a primitive, "unrevised" text.[28] The free editorial activity documented in this chapter shows that what distinguishes W from the

[25]E. C. Colwell, *Studies in Methodology* 45-55.

[26]Linton's description of the supposed revision is no more than a description of scribal tendencies which can be observed in numerous MSS. (Cf. Linton, 351-54.)

[27]Of course in the case of Θ, it appears that these free changes must have been made in its exemplar, or earlier, for Θ's scribe does not appear to have known Greek well enough to have been creative.

[28]Teofilo Ayuso, "¿Texto arrecensional, recensional o prerecensional? Contribución al estudio de la critica textual de los Evangelios," *Est Bib* segunda época 6(1947) 35-90.

Neutral text, the other major body of Egyptian witnesses, can easily be characterized as revisionistic readings. On this score, Lagrange was correct and Ayuso was wrong. In Codex W (and P[45] too) there is unmistakable evidence of a textual tradition which is of secondary value in restoring the original text. W is not a better witness to the original text of Mark, as Ayuso believed. Rather, W demonstrates the effect upon the Markan text of a scribal interest in serving popular religious needs for a clear, easy to read, inoffensive copy of Mark's Gospel.

CHAPTER VII

CONCLUSIONS

The work of textual criticism rarely seems to have advanced by some spectacular and revolutionary leap forward. It is in the nature of the work that progress comes slowly and in small stages. It is, therefore, difficult in any one study to arrive at assured conclusions that are comprehensive in their effect upon textual theory. The more intensive the study the less comprehensive must be the scope, with the result that each piece of scholarly investigation is only one small step, hopefully in the right direction, or one stone in the total edifice. This study has of necessity been limited and specialized. The writer takes some comfort, however, in the belief that solid advance in the overall tasks of textual criticism can be built only upon a carefully-laid and closely-studied foundation made up of the analysis of the NT textual witnesses. This study offers three major conclusions for the continuing work of textual criticism.

AN OBJECTIVE AND THOROUGH METHODOLOGY

The first conclusion of this study is that progress in the formation of an accurate history of the textual transmission of the NT can come only as scholars employ a method of grouping NT witnesses that is objective and complete. This study has argued for, and illustrated the use of, the basic method of establishing quantitative textual relationships proposed by Colwell and Tune as the initial step in characterizing a MS.

Perhaps more than any other topic in textual criticism, the history of research on the Caesarean text illustrates the impasse to which the older methods led. One has only to read the many articles that were produced in the heyday of activity connected with the formation of the Caesarean text theory (roughly 1900-1950) to find the vigorous, but often unproductive, debate over the lists of agreements between MSS. The problem was partially that no one list, nor even the sum of such lists, afforded an accurate view of just how closely a MS was related to the various textual groups of the NT.

The first chapter of this study documents the methodological failures of earlier work, and we present here an example of how helpful a more adequate method can be. All study of the textual relationships of MSS must resort to some tabulation to measure the *amount* of agreement of MSS, but the only reliable way to tell whether the agreement of two MSS is significant is to show the agreement of two MSS in comparison with their disagreement, and their agreement in comparison with the agreement of other representative MSS one with another, Further, such tabulation of agreements must not be a sample, but must be a complete study

85

of the total text, and must be made section by section, since textual affinities in some important MSS vary within individual NT writings.

Codex W agrees with Θ 36.9 percent in Mark 10, for example. But this is meaningful only when one notes the agreement of *all* the representative MSS in that chapter. ℵ and B agree 76.7 percent there. These two MSS are clearly primary witnesses to the same text-type, and their quantitative agreement suggests a criterion for identifying a text-type. It is apparent on the basis of their 36.9 percent agreement that W and Θ do not belong together in the same textual group.

In addition to using the Colwell-Tune method of quantitative analysis, as a suggested second step in proper method we analyzed the individual agreements of MSS in an attempt to *characterize* these agreements. This was done in the belief that the body of readings shared by two MSS is the clearest evidence of what it may be that links them. A characterization of the shared readings of the MSS that appear to be members of the same text group will show the basic nature of that textual group. This characterization of readings was éspecially necessary for the "Caesarean text" because no clear definition of the nature of this text group had been formed.

The agreements of W with each of the other three "Caesarean" representatives—Θ, Fam 13, and P⁴⁵—were characterized in two ways. First, the body of agreements shared by W and *each* of the other named MSS was characterized by noting which representatives of known textual groups most frequently supported the agreements. For example, the most frequent supporter of the W-Θ agreements was Codex D. This fact, plus the fact that Θ shows interesting quantitative agreement with D, means that one can characterize the agreements of W and Θ as readings with strong Western affinity. This is further reinforced when one notes the substantial frequency with which the OL and the Old Syr support the agreements of W and Θ, even when D does not.

Second, we examined the body of variants shared by W and each of the other "Caesareans" to determine what *kinds* of readings they were. Along with this the *significance* of these agreements was studied as to whether there were marks of a special relationship. As a result of this complete procedure, it is possible to make accurate and objective characterizations of the extent and kind of agreement between MSS. Textual critics should no longer use inferior methods of studying textual relationships—methods that are not as thorough as the procedures followed in this study. Unfortunately, some studies still employ the older, inferior methods.[1]

THE TEXTUAL NATURE OF CODEX W

Another conclusion of this study involves the information gathered on the special question of the textual nature of Codex W. We noted that W is not a good supporter of any major text group. It shows almost equal quantitative agreements with the Neutral, Byzantine, and Western representatives, except in Mark 1–4 where W is more clearly Western. The agreement of W with Θ or with 565 throughout Mark

[1]See, e.g., John E. Hartley, "Textual Affinities of Papyrus Bodmer XIV (P⁷⁵)," *EvQ* 40 (1968) 97-102; K. Aland, "Papyrus Bodmer II, ein erster Bericht," *TLZ* 82(1957) 161-84; Victor Martin, ed., *Papyrus Bodmer II, Évangile de Jean, chap. 1–14* (Geneva: 1956).

is far too low to indicate a textual relation other than "Western" textual affinity. This Western influence is so strongly seen in the text of Θ and 565 that these MSS should be regarded as perhaps the second best Greek representatives of the Western text of Mark—second only to Codex Bezae.

The agreement of W with Fam 13 is considerably greater than that of W with Θ or 565. The W-Fam 13 relationship is still not as strong, however, as that of ℵ with B, but it is clear that Fam 13 (much more than 565 or Θ) is related to the text of Codex W. The bulk of the agreements of W with Fam 13 can be characterized as readings with strong Byzantine support. While 565 and Θ are most clearly related to D, Fam 13 is most closely related to the Byzantines in most of Mark. What W has in common with Θ is basically that they share Western readings, with Θ by far the better Western witness over the whole of Mark. What W and Fam 13 have in common is that they share Byzantine readings, with Fam 13 being by far the better Byzantine witness. The distinctive agreements of W with Fam 13 against all the other control witnesses are nearly all readings of an editorial and harmonistic nature.

The relationship of W with P⁴⁵ is stronger still than that of W with Fam 13. The W-P⁴⁵ relationship (68.9%) borders on the 70 percent suggested criterion of a text-type relationship. Their agreements are about evenly supported by the Neutral, Western, and Byzantine representatives, although there does seem to be a slightly greater Neutral element in their agreements. The distinctive W-P⁴⁵ agreements, not shared by the other control witnesses, are basically minor improvements in the Markan text. While there are no striking W-P⁴⁵ agreements, their overall quantitative relationship reveals their close ties.

Our study of the singular readings of W shows the scribal purposes governing the production of its text of Mark. W attempts to eliminate Markan redundancies, to exchange less familiar for more familiar terms, to improve Markan style, to clarify the Markan text by harmonization with Synoptic parallels, and even to alter objectionable statements on the grounds of dogma or tradition. The individual textual character of W is that of a MS prepared for popular reading, for religious edification, and for easy comprehension. One of the important points established in the study of W's singular readings is that such readings show that some scribes exercised noticeable freedom in making their text intelligible for readers. Textual critics must reckon more fully with the fact that a large number of readings were introduced into the MSS not accidentally or as a result of their being found in some exemplar, but as a result of a scribal creativity motivated by certain purposes connected with making the text easy to use in church circles. Scholars must not be too quick to posit a genealogical relationship on the basis of a small number of agreements, especially if those agreements are readings attributable to common and obvious scribal tendencies that could have affected MSS independently.[2]

W is a somewhat carefully produced MS that provides an example of how the text of Mark was shaped for popular Christian tastes in Egypt. Although both

---

[2]Colwell showed how similar purposes in scribes and translators working independently could create the same or similar readings. He noted agreements between readings in the *RSV* of the NT and the singular readings of P⁶⁶, a MS discovered after the RSV was translated! "No one will suggest a genetic kinship here, but if the agreement of P⁶⁶ were with an Old Latin ms . . . ?" (*Studies in Methodology* 124).

Codices B and W are Egyptian MSS, the two must have been prepared for different readers or by scribes with greatly differing concepts of their responsibilities. Codex B, much more frequently than Codex W, contains Markan expressions that are "improved" in Matthew and Luke and in the many later MSS of Mark. For this reason it appears that Codex B was prepared by a scribe who more characteristically valued exact copying even of awkward phrases, while the scribe of Codex W was occupied with the "editorial" interest described above.

THE "PRE-CAESAREAN" TEXT

The third result of this study is a conclusion about the so-called pre-Caesarean text, of which W is supposed to be a leading representative. While this study confirms the close relationship of W with P^{45}, and shows that Fam 13 is a secondary witness to the W-P^{45} text, it also shows that these three witnesses are not related to the Caesarean text represented by 565 or Θ. Further, the agreements that do connect W or P^{45} with 565 or Θ are basically readings resulting from the varying amounts of Western readings in these MSS.[3] The quantity of Western readings in Θ and its allies (565, 700) is so great that the present writer would suggest that perhaps the text represented by these MSS is a form of Western text as it was shaped in the East. The Old Syr, which agrees often with these witnesses, seems to be another such witness to the Western text. The "pre-Caesarean" witnesses are, then, not Caesarean at all.

The W-P^{45} text does not belong to any major text-type. The free scribal activity documented and elaborated in this study was the process that created this distinctive text. Thus it is less than accurate to describe W and P^{45} as "mixed-text" MSS, if by that term one means MSS which were produced by some sort of weaving together of readings from various textual witnesses. Rather, the readings peculiar to W show an editorial treatment of the text of Mark that relied as much on the personal tastes of the scribe as it did upon readings in MSS known to the scribe. As Burkitt said long ago,

> What I doubt is that such correction was always made by means of another roll or codex: I think there were early Christians who thought themselves quite capable of making such corrections by mere instinct, i.e., conjecture, and by their general memory of what the text ought to be.[4]

It is pertinent to ask what the W-P^{45} text was like in the period prior to these witnesses. In the absence of documents from the pre-P^{45} stage of this text one must try to extrapolate intelligently on the basis of available data. We noted in Chapter V of this study that P^{45} is a little closer to B than is W. This evidence can be interpreted to mean (1) that the textual tradition represented by W and P^{45} is basically Neutral, and (2) that this tradition had a stronger Neutral flavor in its

---

[3]Lawrence Allen Eldridge (*The Gospel Text of Epiphanius of Salamis* [SD 41; Salt Lake City: University of Utah, 1969] 124-25) showed that the agreements of the Gospel quotations in Epiphanius with the Caesarean MSS (mainly 28, 565, 700) are in readings supported by a majority of Western witnesses, and he wondered if this Western element has not been underestimated in the previous attempts to analyze the Caesarean group.

[4]"W and Θ," 7.

earlier stages. If this is a reasonable theory of the origin of the W-P^{45} text, what was the course of its further development beyond W?

It is argued here that Fam 13 possibly represents a later development of the text of P^{45} and W. The latter two witnesses show editorial tendencies making Mark more appealing to the popular reader. Fam 13 shows the same editorial tendencies carried to such a point that the text of this witness has comparatively slight agreement with the Neutral witnesses—usually less agreement with them than with the other textual witnesses selected in this study. The W-P^{45} text as represented by Fam 13 not only went farther away from Neutral affiliation but appears to have become a text very similar to the early stages of the Byzantine text.

This study concludes that the designation "pre-Caesarean" should be abandoned as a valid description of W and P^{45}. Codex W and P^{45} do not have a significant relationship with the so-called Caesarean text represented in Θ, and they are in no way an early stage of this text.

Furthermore, the evidence here presented shows that the so-called pre-Caesarean group, the "unrevised" text favored by Ayuso along with the Western text as more original in textual quality, will not furnish the best sources in which to find original Markan readings. Scholars who argue to the contrary must reckon with the imposing evidence that the distinguishing marks of one of the leading witnesses to this "unrevised" text, Codex W in Mark, are readings resulting from free scribal creation. The best source for original Markan readings is the textual tradition that shows greater fidelity to the less elegant Markan expressions. Although they are not flawless, the Neutral textual witnesses appear to be comparatively more reliable as sources for reconstructing the Markan text.[5]

[5]See similar evaluations of the Neutral text by Turner, "Marcan Usage," *JTS* 28(1927) 19, and by Burkitt, "W and Θ," 149-50.

APPENDIX I

MARK 1 — 88 VARIATION-UNITS

	TR	A	ℵ	B	D	W	Θ	565
A	87.5							
ℵ	43.2	40.9						
B	36.4	33.0	72.7					
D	37.5	36.4	34.1	42.1				
W	48.9	43.2	30.7	38.6	44.3			
Θ	46.6	45.5	40.9	43.2	48.7	43.2		
565	45.5	44.3	42.1	37.5	35.2	34.1	54.5	
Fam 13	55.7	51.1	38.6	36.4	38.6	33.0	45.5	69.3

MARK 2 — 69 VARIATION-UNITS

	TR	A	ℵ	B	D	W	Θ	565
A	88.4							
ℵ	44.9	44.9						
B	31.9	34.8	71.0					
D	30.4	31.9	33.3	27.5				
W	26.1	27.5	34.8	30.4	46.8			
Θ	36.2	37.7	47.8	53.6	36.2	26.1		
565	55.1	53.6	55.1	46.4	36.2	24.6	55.1	
Fam 13	68.1	65.2	43.5	30.4	34.8	23.2	39.1	62.3

MARK 3 — 64 VARIATION-UNITS

	TR	A	ℵ	B	D	W	Θ	565
A	79.7							
ℵ	40.6	37.5						
B	45.3	48.4	78.1					
D	28.1	32.8	29.7	21.9				
W	23.4	23.4	28.1	28.1	46.9			
Θ	37.5	43.8	46.9	43.8	32.8	28.1		
565	48.4	54.7	45.3	57.8	29.7	25.0	64.1	
Fam 13	54.7	54.7	39.1	46.9	34.4	28.1	51.6	51.6

MARK 4 — 95 VARIATION-UNITS

	TR	A	ℵ	B	D	W	Θ	565
A	88.4							
ℵ	48.4	55.8						
B	45.3	49.5	78.9					
D	27.4	23.2	25.3	27.4				
W	23.2	26.3	25.3	27.4	57.9			
Θ	38.9	36.8	35.8	34.7	46.3	42.1		
565	41.1	41.4	36.8	31.6	53.7	34.7	76.8	
Fam 13	61.6	56.8	38.9	41.1	30.5	35.8	47.4	55.8

MARK 5 — 84 VARIATION-UNITS

	TR	A	ℵ	B	D	W	Θ	565
A	72.6							
ℵ	53.6	56.0						
B	44.1	57.1	79.8					
D	32.1	21.4	33.3	28.6				
W	42.9	47.6	42.9	45.2	27.4			
Θ	41.7	41.7	46.4	46.4	40.5	33.3		
565	46.4	31.0	34.5	27.4	63.1	36.9	53.6	
Fam 13	51.2	50.0	53.6	52.4	28.6	48.8	48.8	36.9

MARK 6 — 152 VARIATION-UNITS

	TR	A	ℵ	B	D	W	Θ	565
A	88.2							
ℵ	44.1	47.4						
B	48.0	48.7	80.9					
D	42.8	39.5	25.7	33.6				
W	53.9	51.3	36.8	42.8	34.2			
Θ	41.4	40.1	44.7	43.4	42.1	41.4		
565	41.4	40.1	25.7	23.7	60.5	37.5	55.9	
Fam 13	67.1	66.4	43.4	44.1	35.5	61.8	44.1	40.1

MARK 7 — 77 VARIATION-UNITS

	TR	A	ℵ	B	D	W	Θ	565
A	93.5							
ℵ	35.1	33.8						
B	35.1	36.4	80.5					
D	42.9	37.7	33.8	42.9				
W	50.6	46.8	42.9	33.8	50.6			
Θ	41.6	36.4	44.2	49.4	63.6	48.1		
565	51.9	48.1	29.9	37.7	55.8	49.4	70.1	
Fam 13	72.7	70.1	32.5	32.5	49.4	59.7	44.2	48.1

MARK 8 — 100 VARIATION-UNITS

	TR	A	א	B	D	W	Θ	565
A	91.0							
א	52.0	52.0						
B	53.0	53.0	83.0					
D	32.0	35.0	34.0	35.0				
W	34.0	38.0	32.0	29.0	39.0			
Θ	41.0	43.0	33.0	33.0	51.0	41.0		
565	39.0	41.0	35.0	36.0	50.0	40.0	78.0	
Fam 13	53.0	49.0	36.0	31.0	32.0	61.0	43.0	38.0

MARK 9 — 131 VARIATION-UNITS

	TR	A	א	B	D	W	Θ	565
A	89.3							
א	51.9	51.9						
B	48.9	49.6	86.3					
D	42.0	42.7	49.6	45.0				
W	31.3	31.3	38.2	39.7	31.3			
Θ	41.2	37.4	43.5	43.5	42.0	35.1		
565	43.5	41.2	42.7	40.5	37.4	39.7	64.1	
Fam 13	51.9	50.4	31.3	29.8	32.1	53.4	46.6	48.9

MARK 10 — 103 VARIATION-UNITS

	TR	A	א	B	D	W	Θ	565
A	85.4							
א	40.8	39.8						
B	42.7	42.7	76.7					
D	37.9	35.0	32.0	33.0				
W	39.8	47.6	27.2	30.1	42.7			
Θ	26.2	28.2	34.0	31.1	42.7	36.9		
565	35.9	39.8	34.0	25.2	46.6	40.8	74.8	
Fam 13	57.3	62.1	26.2	31.1	36.9	61.2	38.8	46.6

MARK 11 — 85 VARIATION-UNITS

	TR	A	א	B	D	W	Θ	565
A	84.7							
א	43.5	42.4						
B	40.0	47.1	82.4					
D	34.1	34.1	28.2	22.4				
W	42.4	40.0	43.5	43.5	36.5			
Θ	41.2	38.8	31.8	34.1	47.1	41.2		
565	41.2	35.3	29.4	30.6	51.8	44.7	67.1	
Fam 13	62.4	54.1	32.9	34.1	36.5	51.8	44.7	44.7

MARK 12 — 103 VARIATION-UNITS

	TR	A	א	B	D	W	Θ	565
A	87.4							
א	40.8	37.9						
B	39.8	37.9	77.7					
D	31.1	35.0	28.2	31.1				
W	40.8	35.9	37.9	35.9	25.2			
Θ	37.9	35.0	38.8	36.9	41.7	44.7		
565	39.8	35.9	37.9	29.1	51.5	40.8	76.7	
Fam 13	57.3	52.4	35.9	31.1	25.2	54.4	46.6	42.7

MARK 13 — 68 VARIATION-UNITS

	TR	A	א	B	D	W	Θ	565
A	89.7							
א	50.0	48.5						
B	50.0	48.5	77.9					
D	32.4	30.9	32.4	35.3				
W	47.1	42.6	41.2	42.6	32.4			
Θ	35.3	33.8	29.4	19.1	39.7	35.3		
565	36.8	35.3	27.9	26.5	50.0	41.2	76.5	
Fam 13	50.0	57.4	39.7	32.4	25.0	54.4	58.8	54.4

MARK 14 — 149 VARIATION-UNITS

	TR	A	א	B	D	W	Θ	565
A	83.9							
א	53.7	50.3						
B	55.0	55.7	82.6					
D	32.2	29.5	34.9	34.2				
W	42.3	45.0	36.9	38.9	29.5			
Θ	38.3	36.9	31.5	34.9	47.7	34.2		
565	32.2	33.6	27.5	26.8	49.7	40.3	75.2	
Fam 13	47.7	51.7	31.5	36.9	30.2	65.1	47.0	47.0

MARK 15:1 — 16:8 — 71 VARIATION-UNITS

	TR	A	א	B	D	W	Θ	565
A	91.5							
א	60.6	57.7						
B	57.7	62.0	74.6					
D	31.0	31.0	31.0	39.4				
W	36.6	39.4	32.4	36.6	38.0			
Θ	32.4	28.2	31.0	29.6	60.6	39.4		
565	23.9	22.5	25.4	22.5	57.7	32.4	80.3	
Fam 13	67.6	70.4	43.7	53.5	32.4	57.7	39.4	33.8

AGREEMENTS AT 103 VARIATION-UNITS
WHERE P⁴⁵ IS CLEAR

	TR	A	א	B	W	D	P⁴⁵	Θ	565
A	91.3								
א	45.6	45.6							
B	45.6	43.7	84.5						
W	39.8	35.0	34.0	35.0					
D	44.7	44.7	42.7	42.7	39.8				
P⁴⁵	38.8	37.9	36.9	39.8	68.9	39.8			
Θ	43.7	40.8	45.6	43.7	37.9	60.2	36.9		
565	52.4	50.5	42.7	38.8	42.7	56.3	43.7	77.7	
Fam 13	60.2	57.4	27.2	29.1	59.2	44.7	55.3	43.7	48.5

BIBLIOGRAPHY

A. REFERENCE WORKS

Clark, Kenneth W. *A Descriptive Catalogue of Greek Manuscripts in America*. Chicago: University of Chicago Press, 1937.

Metzger, Bruce M. *Annotated Bibliography of the Textual Criticism of the New Testament, 1914-1939*. SD 16. Copenhagen: Munksgaard, 1955.

Moulton, James Hope. *A Grammar of New Testament Greek*, I: *Prolegomena*. 3rd ed. Edinburgh: T. & T. Clark, 1908.

Moulton, James Hope, and Howard, W. F. *A Grammar of New Testament Greek*, II: *Accidence and Word-Formation*. Edinburgh: T. & T. Clark, 1929.

Moulton, James Hope, and Milligan, George. *The Vocabulary of the Greek Testament, Illustrated from the Papyri and other Non-Literary Sources*. London: Hodder & Stoughton, 1930.

Moulton, W. F., and Geden, A. S. *A Concordance to the Greek Testament According to the Texts of Westcott and Hort, Tischendorf and the English Revisers*. 4th ed. revised by H. K. Moulton. Edinburgh: T. & T. Clark, 1963.

B. EDITIONS

Aland, Kurt, ed. *Synopsis Quattuor Evangeliorum*. 2nd ed. Stuttgart: Württembergische Bibelanstalt, 1964.

Beerman, Gustav, and Gregory, Caspar Rene. *Die Koridethi Evangelien*. Leipzig: J. C. Hinrich, 1913.

Belsheim, Johannes. *Das Evangelium des Markus nach dem griechischen Codex aureus Theodorae Imperatricis purpureus Petropolitanus aus dem 9ten Jahrhundert*. In *Christiania Videnskabs-Selskabs Forhandlinger*, 1885, number 9.

Cowper, B. H., ed. *Codex Alexandrinus. Η ΚΑΙΝΗ ΔΙΑΘΗΚΗ. Novum Testamentum Graece ex antiguissimo codice Alexandrino*. London: Williams & Norgate, 1860.

Cronin, H. S. *Codex Purpureus Petropolitanus: The Text of Codex N of the Gospels*. TextS V/4. Cambridge: The University Press, 1899. "Appendix," 106-8.

Kenyon, Frederick G. *The Chester Beatty Biblical Papyri, Descriptions and Texts of Twelve Manuscripts on Papyrus of the Greek Bible*. Fasc. II: *The Gospels and Acts Text*. London: Emery Walker Ltd., 1933.

Lake, Kirsopp, and Lake, Silva. *Family 13 (The Ferrar Group): The Text According to Mark with a Collation of Codex 28 of the Gospels*. SD 11. London: Christophers, 1941.

Legg, S. C. E., ed. *Novum Testamentum Graece, Secundum Textum Westcotto-Hortianum. Evangelium Secundum Marcum*. Oxford: Clarendon, 1935.

Sanders, Henry A. *Facsimile of the Washington Manuscript of the Four Gospels in the Freer Collection*. Ann Arbor: University of Michigan, 1912.

‒‒‒‒‒‒. *The New Testament Manuscripts in the Freer Collection*. University of Michigan Studies, Humanistic Series 9. New York: Macmillan, 1918.

Scrivener, Frederick Henry Ambrose. *Bezae Codex Cantabrigiensis, Being an Exact Copy in Ordinary Type*. Cambridge: Deighton, Bell & Co., 1864.

Tischendorf, Constantinus, ed. *Bibliorum Codex Sinaiticus Petropolitanus. Volumen quartum: Novum Testamentum cum Barnaba et Pastore*. St. Petersburg, 1862.

‒‒‒‒‒‒, ed. *Novum Testamentum Vaticanum, post Angeli Maii aliorumque imperfectos labores ex ipso codice*. Leipzig: Gisecke et Devrient, 1867.

‒‒‒‒‒‒. *Novum Testamentum graece*. Editio octava critica maior. Vol. I. Leipzig: Giesecke et Devrient, 1869.

Wordsworth, John, and White, Henry J. *Novum Testamentum Domini Nostri Iesu Christi Latine*. Vol. I. Oxford: Clarendon, 1889.

Η ΚΑΙΝΗ ΔΙΑΘΗΚΗ. Oxford, 1873. (Textus Receptus).

C. BOOKS AND ARTICLES

Aland, Kurt. "Die griechischen Handschriften des Neuen Testaments," *Materialien zur Neutestamentlichen Handschriftenkunde, I*. Edited by Kurt Aland. Arbeiten zur Neutestamentlichen Textforschung 3. Berlin: De Gruyter, 1969. 1-53.

‒‒‒‒‒‒. "Bemerkungen zu den gegenwärtigen Möglichkeiten textkritischer Arbeit aus Anlass einer Untersuchung zum Cäsarea-text der Katholischen Briefe," *NTS* 17(1970/71) 1-9.

Ayuso, Teofilo. "El texto cesariense del papiro de Chester Beatty en el Evangelio de San Marcos," *Est Bib* 4(1934) 268-81.

‒‒‒‒‒‒. "¿Texto cesariense o precesariense? Su realidad y su trascendencia en la critica textual del Nuevo Testamento," *Bib* 16(1935) 369-415.

‒‒‒‒‒‒. "¿Texto arrecensional, recensional o prerecensional? Contribución al estudio de la Critica Textual de los Evangelios," *Est Bib* segunda época 6(1947) 35-90.

Beasley-Murray, G. R. *A Commentary on Mark Thirteen*. London: Macmillan, 1957.

Birdsall, J. Neville. "The Text of the Gospels in Photius: I," *JTS* N.S. 7(1956) 42-55.

‒‒‒‒‒‒. "The Text of the Gospels in Photius: II," *JTS* N.S. 7(1956) 190-98.

Black, Matthew. *An Aramaic Approach to the Gospels and Acts*. 3rd ed. Oxford: Clarendon, 1967.

Brown, J. Pairman. "An Early Revision of the Gospel of Mark," *JBL* 78(1959) 215-27.

Burkitt, F. C. "Introduction," in P. Mordaunt Bernard, *The Biblical Text of Clement of Alexandria in the Four Gospels and the Acts of the Apostles*. TextS V/5. Cambridge: Cambridge University, 1899. pp. vii-xix.

‒‒‒‒‒‒. *Evangelion Da-Mepharreshe*. Cambridge: Cambridge University, 1904.

‒‒‒‒‒‒. "W and Θ: Studies in the Western Text of St. Mark," *JTS* 17(1916) 1-21, 139-52.

‒‒‒‒‒‒. *Christian Beginnings*. London: University of London, 1924.

‒‒‒‒‒‒. Review of B. H. Streeter, *The Four Gospels*, *JTS* 26(1925) 278-94.

‒‒‒‒‒‒. "The Caesarean Text," *JTS* 30(1929) 347-56.

‒‒‒‒‒‒. "The Chester Beatty Papyri," *JTS* 34(1933) 363-68.

Carder, Muriel M. "A Caesarean Text in the Catholic Epistles," *NTS* 16(1969/70) 252-70.

Clark, Kenneth W. "The Effect of Recent Textual Criticism upon New Testament Studies," *The Background of the New Testament and Its Eschatology*. Edited by W. D. Davies and David Daube. Cambridge: Cambridge University, 1954. 27-51.

Colwell, Ernest C. "External Evidence and New Testament Criticism," *Studies in the History and Text of the New Testament in Honor of Kenneth Willis Clark Ph.D.* Edited by Boyd L. Daniels and M. Jack Suggs. SD 29. Salt Lake City: University of Utah, 1967. 1-12.

_____. *Studies in Methodology in Textual Criticism of the New Testament*. Grand Rapids: Eerdmans, 1969.

Couchoud, Paul-Louis. "Notes sur le texte de St. Marc dans le Codex Chester Beatty," *JTS* 35(1934) 3-22.

Cranfield, C. E. B. *The Gospel According to Saint Mark*. The Cambridge Greek Testament Commentary. Edited by C. F. D. Moule. 3rd impression. Cambridge: Cambridge University, 1966.

Edmunds, A. J. "The Washington Manuscript and the Resurrection in Mark," *Monist* 28(1918) 528-29.

Eldridge, Lawrence Allen. *The Gospel Text of Epiphanius of Salamis*. SD 41. Salt Lake City: University of Utah, 1969.

Epp, Eldon J. *The Theological Tendency of Codex Bezae Cantabrigiensis in Acts*. SNTSMS 3. Cambridge: Cambridge University, 1966.

_____. "The Twentieth Century Interlude in New Testament Textual Criticism," *JBL* 93(1974) 386-414.

_____. "Toward the Clarification of the Term 'Textual Variant,' " in *Studies in New Testament Language and Text*. Edited by J. K. Elliott. Leiden: E. J. Brill, 1976. 153-73.

_____. "The Eclectic Method in New Testament Textual Criticism: Solution or Symptom," *HTR* 69(1976) 211-57.

Faux, A. Review of K. Lake, R. P. Blake, and S. New, "The Caesarean Text of Mark," *Histoire Ecclesiastique*, 26(1930) 119-20.

Fee, Gordon D. *Papyrus Bodmer II (P66): Its Textual Relationships and Scribal Characteristics*. SD 34. Salt Lake City: University of Utah, 1968.

_____. "Codex Sinaiticus in the Gospel of John: A Contribution to Methodology in Establishing Textual Relationships," *NTS* 15(1968/69) 23-44.

Geerlings, Jacob, and New, Silva. "Chrysostrom's Text of the Gospel of Mark," *HTR* 24(1931) 121-42.

Glasson, Thomas Francis. "Did Matthew and Luke Use a 'Western' Text of Mark?" *Exp Tim* 55(1943-44) 180-84.

_____. "An Early Revision of the Gospel of Mark," *JBL* 85(1966) 231-33.

Goodspeed, Edgar J. "The Freer Gospels," *AJT* 18(1914) 131-46, 266-81.

_____. *The Freer Gospels*. Historical and Linguistic Studies 3. Chicago: University of Chicago, 1914.

Grant, F. C. "Studies in the Text of St. Mark," *ATR* 20(1938) 103-19.

Greenlee, J. Harold. *The Gospel Text of Cyril of Jerusalem*. SD 17. Copenhagen: Munksgaard, 1955.

Gregory, Caspar Rene. *Das Freer-Logion*. Leipzig: J. C. Hinrich, 1908.

Griffith, John G. "Numerical Taxonomy and Some Primary MSS of the Gospels," *JTS* N.S. 20(1969) 389-406.

Hauck, D. Friedrich. *Das Evangelium des Markus*. THKNT. Leipzig: A. Deichertsche Verlagsbuchhandlung, 1931.

Hawkins, John C. *Horae Synopticae*. 2nd revised ed. Oxford: Clarendon, 1909.

Hedley, P. L. "The Egyptian Texts of the Gospels and Acts," *CQR* 118(1934) 23-39, 188-230.

Hills, Edward F. "Harmonizations in the Caesarean Text of Mark," *JBL* 66(1947) 135-52.

_____. "The Inter-Relationship of the Caesarean Manuscripts," *JBL* 68(1949) 141-59.

_____. "A New Approach to the Old Egyptian Text," *JBL* 69(1950) 345-62.

Hoskier, H. C. "The New Codex 'W,' " *Expositor* VIII/5 (1913) 467-80, 515-31.

_____. *Codex B and Its Allies: A Study and An Indictment*. 2 vols. London: Bernard Quaritch, 1914.

_____. "A Note on 'Eastern' and 'Caesarean' Texts," *Bulletin of the Bezan Club* 5(1928) 13-21.

_____. "Some Study of P⁴⁵ with Special Reference to the Bezan Text," *Bulletin of the Bezan Club* 12 (1937) 51-57.

Huffman, Norman. "Suggestions from the Gospel of Mark for a New Textual Theory," *JBL* 56(1937) 347-59.

Huston, Hollis W. "Mark 6 and 11 in P⁴⁵ and in the Caesarean Text," *JBL* 74(1955) 262-71.

Jacquier, E. "Le manuscrit Washington des Évangiles," *RB* 22(1913) 547-55.

Kenyon, Frederick G. *Recent Developments in the Textual Criticism of the Greek Bible.* London: Oxford University, 1933.

_____. "Some Notes on the Chester Beatty Gospels and Acts," *Quantulacumque, Studies Presented to Kirsopp Lake.* Edited by R. P. Casey, S. Lake, and A. K. Lake. London: Christophers, 1937. 145-48.

_____. "The Western Text in the Gospels and Acts," *Proceedings of the British Academy* 24(1938) 287-315.

_____. Review of K. and S. Lake, *Family 13 (The Ferrar Group)*, *JTS* 43(1942) 94-98.

_____. *Our Bible and the Ancient Manuscripts.* Revised ed. New York: Harper, 1958.

Kilpatrick, G. D. "The Gentile Mission in Mark and Mark 13:9-11," *Studies in the Gospels.* Edited by D. E. Nineham. Oxford: Basil Blackwell, 1967. 145-58.

Kretzmann, P. E. "The Freer Manuscripts and the Oxyrhynchus Papyri," *Theological Monthly* 1(1921) 255-59.

_____. "The Koridethi Manuscript and the Latest Discoveries in Egypt," *CTM* 3(1932) 574-78.

Klijn, A. F. J. *A Survey of the Researches into the Western Text of the Gospels and Acts.* Utrecht: Drukkerij v. h. Kemink En Zoon N.V., 1949.

_____. "A Survey of the Researches into the Western Text of the Gospels and Acts," *NovT* 3(1959) 1-27, 161-73.

_____. *A Survey of the Researches into the Western Text of the Gospels and Acts: Part Two 1949-1969.* NovTSup 21. Leiden: E. J. Brill, 1969.

Lagrange, M. J. "Le group dit césaréen des manuscrits des Évangiles," *RB* 38(1929) 481-512.

_____. *Évangile selon Saint Marc.* 4th ed. Paris: Librairie Lecoffre; 1966(1929).

_____. "Les Papyrus Chester Beatty pour les Évangiles," *RB* 43(1934) 5-41.

Lake, Kirsopp. *Codex 1 of the Gospels and Its Allies.* TextS VII/3. Cambridge: Cambridge University Press, 1902.

Lake, Kirsopp, and Blake, R. P. "The Text of the Gospels and the Koridethi Codex," *HTR* 16(1923) 267-86.

Lake, Kirsopp, Blake, R. P., and New, Silva. "The Caesarean Text of the Gospel of Mark," *HTR* 21(1928) 207-404.

Lake, Kirsopp. *The Text of the New Testament.* 6th ed. revised by Silva New. London, 1928; repr. London: Rivington's, 1959.

Lake, Kirsopp, and Lake, Silva. "De Westcott et Hort au Père Lagrange et au-dela," *RB* 48(1939) 497-505.

Lake, Kirsopp, and Lake, Silva. "The Byzantine Text of the Gospels," *Mémorial Lagrange.* Paris, 1940. 251-58.

Lake, Silva. *Family Pi and the Codex Alexandrinus.* SD 5. London: Christophers, 1937.

Linton, Olof. "Evidences of a Second Century Revised Edition of St. Mark's Gospel," *NTS* 14(1967/68) 321-55.

Metzger, Bruce M. *Chapters in the History of New Testament Textual Criticism.* NTTS 4. Grand Rapids: Eerdmans, 1963.

_____. *Historical and Literary Studies: Pagan, Jewish, and Christian.* NTTS 8. Leiden: E. J. Brill, 1968.

————. *The Text of the New Testament*. 2nd ed. New York: Oxford University, 1968.

Moule, C. F. D. *An Idiom-Book of New Testament Greek*. 2nd ed. Cambridge: Cambridge University, 1963.

Murphy, Harold R. "Eusebius' New Testament Text in the *Demonstratio Evangelica*," *JBL* 73(1954) 162-68.

Phillips, C. A. " 'The Washington MS of the Gospels' by Dr. Streeter," *Bulletin of the Bezan Club* 5(1928) 9-12.

————. "The Caesarean Text, with Special Reference to the New Papyrus and Another Ally," *Bulletin of the Bezan Club* 11(1932) 5-19.

Pryke, E. J. *Redactional Style in the Marcan Gospel*. SNTSMS 33. Cambridge: Cambridge University, 1978.

Robertson, A. T. "Some Interesting Readings in the Washington Codex," *Expositor* IX/3 (1925) 192-98.

Sanders, H. A. "Recent Text Studies in the New Testament," *ATR* 16(1934) 266-82.

————. "The Egyptian Text of the Four Gospels and Acts," *HTR* 26(1933) 77-98.

Souter, Alexander. "The Freer (Washington) MS of the Gospels," *Expositor* VIII/8(1914) 350-67.

————. "The Koridethi Gospels," *Expositor* VIII/10 (1915) 173-81.

Streeter, Burnett Hillman. *The Four Gospels*. 2nd impression. London: Macmillan, 1926.

————. "The Caesarean Text of the Gospels," *JTS* 26(1925) 373-78.

————. "The Washington MS and the Caesarean Text of the Gospels," *JTS* 27(1926) 144-47.

————. "The Washington MS of the Gospels," *HTR* 19(1926) 165-72.

————. "Origen, ℵ and the Caesarean Text," *JTS* 36(1935) 178-80.

————. "The Caesarean Text of Matthew and Luke," *HTR* 28(1935) 231-35.

————. "Codices 157, 1071 and the Caesarean Text," *Quantulacumque, Studies Presented to Kirsopp Lake*. Edited by R. P. Casey, S. Lake, and A. K. Lake. London: Christophers, 1937. 149-50.

Suggs, M. Jack. "The Eusebian Text of Matthew," *NovT* 1(1956) 233-45.

————. "Eusebius and the Gospel Text," *HTR* 50(1957) 307-10.

Swete, Henry Barclay. *The Gospel According to St. Mark*. 3rd ed. London: Macmillan, 1909.

Tarelli, C. C. "Some Linguistic Aspects of the Chester Beatty Papyrus of the Gospels," *JTS* 29(1938) 254-59.

————. "The Chester Beatty Papyrus and the Caesarean Text," *JTS* 40(1939) 46-55.

————. "The Chester Beatty Papyrus and the Western and Byzantine Texts," *JTS* 41(1940) 253-60.

————. "Some Further Linguistic Aspects of the Chester Beatty Papyrus of the Gospels," *JTS* 43(1942) 19-25.

Tasker, R. V. G. "The Quotations from the Synoptic Gospels in Origen's *Exhortation to Martyrdom*," *JTS* 36(1935) 60-65.

————. "The Text Used by Eusebius in *Demonstratio Evangelica* in Quoting from Matthew and Luke," *HTR* 28(1935) 61-69.

————. "The Readings of the Chester Beatty Papyrus in the Gospel of St. John," *JTS* 36(1935) 387-91.

————. "The Text of the Fourth Gospel Used by Origen in His *Commentary on John*," *JTS* 37(1936) 146-55.

————. "The Chester Beatty Papyrus and the Caesarean Text of Luke," *HTR* 29(1936) 345-52.

————. "The Chester Beatty Papyrus and the Caesarean Text of John," *HTR* 30(1937) 157-64.

_____. "The Text of St. Matthew Used by Origen in His *Commentary on St. Matthew*," *JTS* 38(1937) 60-64.

Taylor, Vincent. *The Gospel According to St. Mark*. 2nd ed. London: Macmillan, 1966.

Thrall, Margaret E. *Greek Particles in the New Testament*. NTTS 3. Leiden: E. J. Brill, 1962.

Turner, C. H. "Marcan Usage: Notes, Critical and Exegetical, on the Second Gospel," *JTS* 25(1924) 377-86; 26(1925) 12-20, 145-56, 225-40, 337-46; 27(1926) 58-62; 28(1927) 9-30, 349-62; 29(1928) 275-89, 346-61.

_____. "A Textual Commentary on Mark 1," *JTS* 28(1927) 145-58.

_____. "Western Readings in the Second Half of St. Mark's Gospel," *JTS* 29(1928) 1-16.

Vaganay, Leon. *Initiation à la critique textuelle néo-testamentaire*. Paris, 1934.

Wallace-Hadrill, D. S. "Eusebius and the Gospel Text of Caesarea," *HTR* 49(1956) 105-14.

White, A. H. "The Problem of the Caesarean Text," *Journal of the Manchester University Egypt and Oriental Society* 24(1942-45; published in 1947) 39-59.

Williams, C. S. C. "Syriasms in the Washington Text of Mark," *JTS* 42(1941) 177-78.

D. UNPUBLISHED MATERIAL

Baikie, James E. McA. "The Caesarean Text *Inter Pares*." Unpublished M.Litt. dissertation, Cambridge University, 1936.

Fee, Gordon D. "The Significance of Papyrus Bodmer II and Papyrus Bodmer XIV-XV for Methodology in New Testament Textual Criticism." Unpublished Ph.D. dissertation, University of Southern California, 1966.

Hills, Edward F. "The Caesarean Family of New Testament Manuscripts." Unpublished Th.D. dissertation, Harvard Divinity School, 1946.